ON AND ON

Joe Cooper

Dedication

Special thanks to my family for all the love and support they give me

.

ON and ON

Copyright

Published by: Book Publish Pro

<u>ON and ON</u>

I was 22 years old the first time I died. There have been several "near-death" experiences since. Otherwise, I'm a very average guy, a little under six foot tall and about 190 pounds, stocky, athletic build, size ten shoe, light-complected with light brown hair, sometimes reddish in the sun. Physically very unremarkable.

Not a genius, no photographic memory. I do read people's body language uncommonly well, but that's more of a learned skill. I can fight but not a pugilist, can shoot but not a marksman, and can speak several languages, again more of a learned skill; I am athletic but not a pro, and I'm good at most athletic activities. I love to sing but cannot play an instrument. Been told I'm boyishly handsome. I think I'm damn funny. But who doesn't? I'm self-sufficient. I can cook and build shit.

I'm a sucker for a sad story, love a good Western novel and any Elvis movie, love sports, fuck it up whenever in Vegas, and sometimes place a sports bet. If I were your neighbor, I'd be the cool, handsome guy you're secretly jealous of and hate a little inside.

But a closer, extended look will show that nothing is average about me. I heal very, very fast; I Don't age, and mentally, I am a rock (seen crazy shit), and I met Jesus. He was unmistakably engaging. I listened to him talk more than once and was fascinated by what he had to say. He was a little self-righteous, but I get it (maybe it's not a great joke).

That's what I wrote in my very first social media post. I don't know why I wanted to share, but after two thousand-plus years, I was through hiding who I was. Who knew if anyone would even read it? I had no friends or followers, and I barely understood how to use any social platform, but that shit went viral in four days. The comments ranged from "You're going to hell!!" to, "I think I met you at the Alamo!"

For the record, I am in a living hell of sorts already. I was not in Texas at that time in history. Sixty or so years before the Alamo, I did ride with some badass Texas rangers in the late 1860s chasing wild, bloodthirsty, crazy renegade Comanche Indians (I will share that story momentarily).

I was so beyond caring who knew what about me. I had tried for the last fifty years not to be photographed or videotaped (damn near impossible since iPhones and ring doorbells.) I am social and have never been the type to live like a recluse; I figured what the fuck. The world is loaded with crazies, and honestly, it always has been. I've seen complete lunacy in the name of scientific discoveries and government overreach. Nations go to war over democratic ideologies and religion. Religion, in my opinion, is the biggest evil in the history of humanity. Not God, but the self-righteous assholes willing to send millions of peasants to die for their interpretation of what God or Allah tells them. It's timeless and breaks across race and country. It happens everywhere and has been a constant theme throughout my lifetime. Times change, ideas change, and surprisingly enough, facts change. People thought tomatoes were poisonous, believed the world was flat (sorry, flat earthers), or that smoking was good for you. Some people believe the mob didn't shoot JFK, that Tupac Shakur is still alive, and that we didn't land on the moon. Some people think that a secret society runs our global economy. So, not thinking anyone could give a rat's ass about one more lunatic. Here we are. Writing my autobiography would not only kill time and give me a mental outlet but also allow me to be a part of the global community and have a voice (personal growth.)

After my initial post and reading several thousand comments, I waited a week and started telling my story. I switched my platform to a blog. (Eventually, to this book you are reading.) It was easier to ramble without a word count limit. I didn't care who believed me. I could still be anonymous. People could read it as fiction for all I cared. I've been carrying this burden and had to expel it from my brain. I used the username ForeverMan356.

I'm neither a vampire nor a superhero; this is not an origin story. It's just what happened to me. I have no idea why I've experienced this life; I didn't sell my soul to the devil, nothing bit me, nor was I exposed to any funky substance. If any of those things happened to me, at least my story would be a great comic book. I understand that I am special. I'm one hundred percent sure that this is a fucking curse and far from a gift. The pain of being alone is unbearable. Watching friends and family die is far worse than the gift of immortality. Creating lie after lie to describe myself and add a make-believe personal history gets old and confusing. Was I a plumber or a lawyer? (Never a lawyer; nobody in history likes them.) Was I born in Ireland or France? (Never France, not arrogant enough.) Was I married? (Not married cuts off too many possibilities.) You get it.

ON and ON

After several posts, I received sponsorship offers from companies like LifeLock, Red Bull, and Dos Equis. I don't need the money but shit, who doesn't want to be sponsored? My goal was not to be famous. Who the hell wants to be a Kardashian? I wanted to be honest for once. I want to give some real insight into true history from someone living it. Not what a broken piece of old pottery found on the floor instead of on a table might suggest. There is no extrapolation, only facts. I want to tell a story in a fun way, my way. I will use pop culture terms from the last eighty or so years so as not to make you wonder, "What the fuck is he talking about."

Life, until very recently, was very expendable. Families had kids every year. There are many reasons why. No birth control is one reason, and we all know people love to fuck. Another reason is that more prominent families succeeded in the family business, with more helping hands to get the job done. But a huge reason is also that most children die. Some parents did not grow close bonds with their children until they were older, so it would hurt less when that child died. Families gave children away because they couldn't feed them, sold them, or killed daughters. People lived in shit. Actual shit because they didn't understand sanitation. No one bathed. I only know the Japanese culture of washing regularly (I know this because I read James Clavell's Shogun novel). People were always sick. So many things could kill you. Stepping in a hole and twisting your ankle could lead to a blood disease, and you'd be dead within the year.

I knew a guy whose finger got infected from biting his nails too low; that minor injury turned into an MRSA-type disease, and he died. Byron Carter, An automobile innovator, stopped to help a lady with car problems. Vehicles didn't include electric starters yet; cars had to be hand-cranked to start. He inserted the hand crank into the slot just below the grill and pulled it firmly. The engine backfired, causing the steel hand crank to reverse its swing and smash into Carter's jaw, breaking it. His broken jaw wasn't life-threatening, but the subsequent infection turned into pneumonia, and he died a week later. Life was generally short and unfulfilling.

Historians write about the history of this and that, but I lived it. I obviously can't tell you about every society that ever existed, but I can tell you simple things that historians only guess about. For example, Michelangelo was a complete weirdo. No one liked the strange asshole. Da Vinci was the most intelligent, remarkable, and down-to-earth person I ever met. He also did weird shit all the time but somehow made it work, like always writing words backward and doing it so quickly that we invented a drinking game based on who could decipher the words first. Sometimes changed languages and laughed as we fumbled, trying to figure it out. Another thing about Da Vinci is he never slept. His mind was always on overdrive. A close second was Ben Franklin. Ben was also a little crazy and did not give a fuck about anything unless it was his current project or pussy. He loved women. All shapes, sizes, and all colors, and he adored older women. (Ben always said they were less work.) He made a herbal drink that tasted like shit but provided a rock-hard boner; the original Viagra. He was banging high-society French women well into his seventies. Ben was always singularly minded towards figuring out how the universe worked, one project at a time. I could go on forever about the great men we all know, assholes who became famous, tyrants who

ON and ON

were in charge by birth but also riddled with congenital disabilities and insanity. Fuck all those guys; it's the great men that history never knew that I would try to write about. I have hundreds of stories about some of the unknown, never written about men who crossed my path; many I have forgotten, but some will never leave my memories. I'm not going to tell my story in chronological order. It'll be more of how stories get told while drinking beer around a campfire as I feel them or a tangent that reminds me of something that leads to something else. It will not be Stienbeckish, taking three pages to describe a turtle crossing a dusty road, just the facts I remember. Mostly true but often embellished for dramatic or humorous effect. An excellent and believable lie will likely also be thrown in. I also want to add before I begin that when I was in a committed relationship, I was always monogamous. When I was a single man, I had all the hormones of a twenty-two-year-old man, so try to remember that before you judge me too harshly about any mention of my many relationships.

Well Shit, here we go:

The best place to start is the beginning.

TABLE OF CONTENTS

ON and ON

The Sailfish

I have many memories of being a child living with my family. I can't, unfortunately, recall my mother's face; I sometimes see a shadowy glimpse of her in a dream, a dream I often have and quickly try to go back to sleep and continue the dream after I see her, but it's continually lost at the exact moment right before I get to her. I did have a wife. (Many wives over the years.) The first one I loved deeply. She was sweet and caring. Our family was poor but hard-working, and I did not give her the credit she deserved. While I plowed fields, she did everything else and saw to my every need. We had no children. I blamed her, but obviously, it was my seed, not swimming. I was angry at her for not providing me with a child. I said mean shit to her far too often, and I feel very ashamed of my words and behaviors directed toward her. I was an asshole.

Our household contained many people from our extended family. Several tiny houses were loosely connected on the corners of the family's property. I could see every house from my front door. Everyone was within yelling distance. Aunts, uncles, and cousins were all connected. Elders lived, worked, and died in the same dark, sod-roofed huts where we all lived. My mom's parents, Gran and Pop, lived in the same house with my parents, brother, me, and my wife.

I have the most memories of my younger brother. We spent most of our days together. He was a little less than two years younger. We were very different but somehow the same. At a young age, he was already taller than me. He was much darker complected than me. We looked very similar with subtle differences; my eyes and hair were lighter, but he was primarily a bigger version of me, like the bigger SUVs in the same automobile class. I liked to joke and sometimes procrastinate. He was more serious and always doing things the right way. His humor would come from a different angle than mine. He saw the world just a degree or two differently than I did. No one has ever made me laugh as hard as he did. His unseen-by-me perspective would always hit me deep in my funny bone.

I would bicker and butt heads with our father, but he never did. He was more of a gentle giant. His name was Jareth, which translates to "the gentle one" (Something my parents got right). I was hot-headed and looking for provocation to fight. He was a protector; I was rebellious.

I had a great relationship with my grandfather. I called him Pop. He was a large man with giant wrinkled hands; he was known for his humor and strength. He kept his gray hair and beard short. We had the same shade of green, sometimes bluish eyes. He was patient with me and my brother and made me feel important. He was always available for council; his wisdom should have been more important to me. (I was always hard-headed.)

My Gran was gray, frail, sharp-tongued, witty, and eccentric. She would make outlandish jokes and claims. I never knew if what she said was truthful or some bullshit she had fabricated. She was by far the most prolific and fantastic liar I have encountered. She somehow made every statement feel true. She told me, "Goats always face the same direction on a hill because two of their legs are shorter." When I showed her goats facing in different directions, She, without pause, said, "Honey, those are the cheese goats. You can't make cheese without them." It sounded perfectly reasonable to my six-year-old mind. She also once told me, "There are more trees on earth than stars in the sky." Surprisingly enough, that's a true statement. (I don't know how she knew that shit, maybe when you throw enough shit against a wall, some sticks.) If I wanted an accurate answer to my questions about the world, I should ask someone else. She always wore a long gray braid pulled back tight, the same tattered dress, and never wore shoes. Even in the winter, she was barefooted, she claimed, "I came into this world without shoes, and I'll die without them."

My Pop and Gran had daily chores but spent most of their days in a coupled existence. You rarely saw one without the other. They had a love I wouldn't fully understand for over a thousand years. I felt like she was crazy and he was a saint. My mother would say, "My father was a tyrant as a young man, brash and mean when he drank. He drank far too often. He would leave for months, fighting silly skirmishes with some Pictish clans. He is making amends to her for his previous behaviors."

I had heard the stories about my Pop's bravery and savage fighting prowess. As I got older, I would inquire about those stories, but he was always vague and usually answered, "Dat, my boy, was another life, which I'd like to forget."

I never saw him drink alcohol. I never heard him say an unkind word to my Gran. My Dad did not dare raise his voice towards my Pop. He must have been a badass because my Dad yelled at everyone else except my Gran.

Throughout my youth, my Pop was always trying to teach me lessons. We would build things together. Once a small canoe. The process seemed overwhelming to me at the beginning. I had to chop the giant oak tree down, debranch it, and then begin to cut and hollow it out. I lost patience with building it several times. I'd half-ass my efforts only to see Pop drop his head and walk away. He provided many helpful tips but never actually did any physical labor. I decided to quit several times, but he always wrangled me back in to finish it. Jareth was eager to help. I let him chop and saw away when I was tired or bored. I had a great deal of pride in the finished product. (Jareth did most of the actual work.) We used it to fish in a small pond on our land. Jareth used it much more than I did. I had a small attention span and would only fish briefly; Jareth could spend hours on that small pond and catch nothing but be content with his efforts. I lost interest in the canoe shortly after we were finished. Jareth used it for years. (I still called it my canoe.)

Pop and I made a small dagger with a hard wooden handle. I was very proud of that knife. Pop called it a *Sgian Dubh.* The actual translation is a 'hidden knife.' Scotsman would hide them just under their kilts. It can also be called a dirk. I used it daily to do my chores. (I also cut myself with it several times.) It only had a small six-inch blade but took days to forge. I had no problem with beating that metal for hours. (Anger issues.) A couple of years after making the boat, I was a touch more mature, and the knife was my cherished belonging. I loved being in our blacksmithing hut. The heat coming from the crucible called to me. Picturing the tree trunk that would become the canoe was easy, and having the vision to change a hunk of material into a completely

ON and ON

new object through hard work intrigued me. I loved all of the tools used to make my little dirk. I spent many hours hamming metal with Pop over our years together. I would eventually become efficient, smithing everything needed for our farm. I made a leather sheath to not only hold my new blade but also to display it. (I wasn't concealing shit.)

The family went to town for the annual spring festival just weeks after my dirk was completed. The festival was always a great event, including horseracing and entertainment troops. Merchants would bring items to be bought and traded. We brought excess wheat and seeds to sell. There were also bare-knuckle boxing matches. No prize money was awarded, but the honor of winning was priceless. My father and uncles fought every year that I could remember. Each clan would have a couple of men represented to compete. Everyone from miles around would come to watch the fights. There were no timed rounds; two men entered a circle marked in the dirt. The match only ended when either one man quit (which rarely happened) or he was unable to continue. Knocked out or injured. The crowd would gather to watch. Me and Jareth sat in a tree with most of the other boys who had also come to watch their relatives fight for glory and honor. Men placed side bet wagers, some for money, some for materials, and some in exchange for work. An intelligent, poorer man could barter from work to coins in his pocket. Pop always had a few coins saved for the annual event.

Last year's champion, a giant, perfidious, ugly man from Clan Robertson, had the right to choose his first opponent. He decided on a thin, weakly dark horse champion from Clan Dunbar. The champion entered the ring to applause and sneers. Our clan was not a big fan of any Dunbar, but we disliked the Robertson man more. This giant of a man fought dirty and was generally considered an asshole. He had broken my uncle's jaw two years prior and spat on him when he couldn't continue. (We hated that fucker.) Clan Robertson came out arrogant and cocky; he walked around the circle antagonizing his opponent. He turned and pulled up his kilt showing him his bare arse. He stood before the Dunbar man and stuck his hairy chin out to show him how unafraid and unchallenged he thought the fight would end. Dunbar gave him a quick slap to his smirk. Hard, but not devastating. He suddenly applied two more brutal open-handed slaps to each side of the big man's face. This time, drawing blood from his nose. Robertson was furious and grabbed the more petite man and threw him out of the circle. Spectators helped Dunbar back inside the ring, but Robertson tried a dirty left hook before the two men were reset.

Dunbar saw it coming and stepped out of range just in time, then replaced his steps and brought a straight right hand to the hulking man's repugnant face. The quick punch stumbled him, and the smaller, speedier man was on him in less than a second, raining blow after blow in a whirlwind of wild and precisely aimed punches. The Dunbar man won. Robertson showed some class by raising the small man's hand and embracing him in a big bear hug. I saw Pop walk over and collect several coins from a not-so-happy bystander. My father fought a one-sided win over an older gentleman well past his prime fighting days. After the big upset fight, all the rest of the bouts were generally forgetful.

ON and ON

As Jareth and I made our rounds checking out the rest of the festival, several older boys accosted us. It was just juvenile fun for them; they were bullying all the younger boys, and we were next in line. The identical group of boys almost got us last season. It had happened to us several years in a row, but nothing terrible usually happened. We would run away and try to avoid them. This time, however, I was caught and held down, and they stole my newly forged knife. I remember crying as they pushed me back to the ground and walked away with it. I had thrown several punches to no avail; Jareth had tried to help me but was quickly restrained and wasn't helpful at all. We walked back to our family group, and I was clearly upset. My Dad was busy celebrating his victory, so just the woman and Pop were gathered together. Immediately, Pop asked, "Have you been crying? What happened?" I told him the story. He looked at me and, dead-faced, said, "Go get your fecking knife back." He had never cursed at me before.

"There are four of them, and they are older and bigger than me." I tried to explain, looking for sympathy.

"I don't recall asking you who or what they are; go get what is yours."

The way he spoke to me scared me. I wanted to please him. If my Dad would have said the exact words to me, the effect would have been very different. I loved and respected Pop; I craved his approval. I walked slowly back to where I knew to find them. I didn't have a plan. I just knew I wasn't going back to face my grandfather without my knife. They saw me coming and stopped what they were doing to berate me with insults.

"Here comes the crier."

8

"Little baby, come back for another ass beating?"

"I'd just like my knife back, please," I pleaded.

"If you want it, come take it," the biggest boy countered. With my hands open and facing him, I walked up with my head down. He pushed my hands away and punched me harder than I had ever been hit, cutting the brow above my left eye. Blood immediately streamed down my face and into both eyes. Something suddenly awakened inside me, and I was no longer afraid of him. I was furious. I saw red, as the saying goes. I remembered how the Dunbar man had attacked the Roberston guy. I threw myself at the bully. I must have caught him unexpectedly because he was not ready for my assault. I don't remember much; it's all kind of a blur, but while I was on top of him throwing wild punches, the knife fell to his side. I saw it and urgently grabbed it. I jumped off of him, knife in hand, and ran. I ran faster than I had ever run. I don't know if they chased me. I didn't look back. Thinking back to that moment, I wonder why I didn't try to stab him or at least turn and face them with my weapon pointed in their direction. I just needed my knife back so Pop would be proud of me. When I returned, everyone was already walking back to our farm. Only Pop had waited for me. I walked to him and proudly showed him my reward. He didn't say a word to me. He tossed me a cloth to clean my face and walked away. What? No, well done. No atta boy? No, I'm proud of you. As I followed, It crushed me. Then, after about halfway home, I realized I didn't need any words of praise. I had faced my fears, stood up for myself, and had righted a wrong bestowed upon me. The pip returned to my step. I had accomplished something important that I may not have understood if Pop had acknowledged it verbally. I had

ON and ON

learned a lesson that I would use repeatedly throughout my lifetime. I would never let anyone take advantage of me again. I caught up with my Pop, grabbed his hand, and asked him, "Why did you bet on the Dunbar man? Don't we hate them?"

"Hate is a strong word. I prefer, but I don't generally care for, the Dunbars. I fought side by side with that man's Dad several times. Lanky and shifty, he was. I also prefer a little coin in my pocket when I have an edge betting."

My Gran died in the early morning just before our next summer harvest. It was the first family death that I was old enough to understand. I have no idea how old she was. She felt old to me then, but everyone is old when you're twelve. That morning, she wasn't at the hearth preparing breakfast with Mom. I was shocked when Pop entered the room with tears streaming down his face. I had never seen him cry before. He said, "She is gone." He walked out into the sunrise. Gran hadn't been sick; I didn't know she was ill. We burned her body that evening, and I saw Pop drunk for the first time. I didn't like it. He was an asshole to everyone. I left and went to bed. Three weeks later, Pop died. I guess he just gave up. I think of him often and smile about the many things in life he taught me, timeless treasures of knowledge that grandfathers bestow upon their grandchildren.

I am Celtic by birth, born in Caledonia, Scotland. I do still have a bit of a Scottish accent. I will sometimes say *"fek" instead of fuck*. I believe my lack of passiveness can be attributed to my lineage. (I sometimes need a reason why being a dick isn't my fault.) I lived on our family farm. We grew wheat and potatoes along with various other vegetables. It was a challenging but honest life. I will never forget the long, hard days spent behind our oxen tilling the rocky fields. I dream of those days, too. Why I dream about plowing a field with the most technologically obscure device is insane, but that small memory is stuck in my subconscious. I sometimes daydream about introducing a tractor to my father and love to think about his possible reactions. Knowing my Dad, he would have found a reason to hate it or blame me for some wrongdoing. (I still have daddy issues.)

The small memory of plowing our fields reminds me of everything I didn't know about the world. A much simpler time: early to bed, getting up before the sun, working all day in the field with my brother, eating, making love to my wife, and doing it all over again. I didn't have dreams of anything better. We were solid and secure in our life. I want to tell you every day was bliss, but that'd be a bold-faced lie. I was hard to get along with and wanted things my way. I was the worst fish in the sea- The Sailfish. My father was always on my ass, and I gave him every reason. There wasn't anything physically special about my father. He had a massive salad of bright red hair and a bushel of jabbing coarse spikes of beard hair sticking out of his face. He was lean and mean. His anger would spew like a volcano with hot lava insults directed at everyone and no one, but mostly at me. I inherited his temper. Everyone in his vicinity would back away when he erupted, but I was drawn closer to the conflict and stood in the tornado's path. We never had a physical altercation, close a couple of times, but our words flew like daggers and ninja stars at each other, inflicting much more pain than any punch. All I know is that I was unable to cower before his anger. It challenged me to fight back. I felt someone had to stand up to him and declared myself the family responder. Hopefully, he respected my courage, but he would probably say something like, "Only a stupid man treats his ignorance as bravery." (Say it in a harsh Scottish accent to get the full meaning.)

If not for my brother, I would have left. I've had years to ponder and self-analyze why I behaved so horribly. All I can say is I was angry, but I don't know why. (It was Dad, couldn't it be me?) I was full of myself and thought I was smarter than everyone else. Smarter about what? No fucking idea! I've changed a lot since those days (but I still really like myself.)

Our small village was all I knew about life. There was a small township area where goods were bought and sold. Annual events, such as small festivals, were held, and traveling troops of entertainers would sometimes stop. It had a small tavern but only a little more. My family rarely went into town more than once or twice a year. As I got older, my trips became more frequent, but only to buy supplies the farm needed. My father once decided to add sheep to our farm and try to breed and sell them. That Idea lasted a little more than two seasons. Sheep may have been the only animal more stubborn than him on the planet. They broke out of pens and ate half of our wheat field. I was constantly hunting strays and once found one roaming five miles away. Some days, there were five extra sheep, and some days, ten were missing. Bears ate them. They were a pain in the ass; it was a fiasco. I've never seen my father madder than when my mother asked him if they were worth the effort. (They were not, and he knew it.) He just hated the thought of failure. He finally told me to round them up and sell them in town. He only wanted enough seed to replant the fields they had eaten. I passed the problem on to another farmer with bright hopes of sheep ranching. Did you know sheep will eat everything in a field down to pulling the roots out? After they have fed, a field will be useless for several seasons. We found that out the hard way.

I didn't know about wealth or poverty. I learned about family and clans. Growing up, we were aware of the theft, fights, and sometimes murders occurring; even so, our little community was safe, and everyone somewhat stayed to themselves or with their family or clan. Bitter arguments did happen, and, in some cases, generational hate existed. Jareth and I were never allowed to speak to anyone in the Dunbar clan. No idea why, and it sucked because there were two hot fucking Dunbar sisters our age; we always eye fucked them.

There were always scuffles and rivalries between clans, mostly about nonsense, and no one usually died. Crimes and murder did happen; it just wasn't a regular occurrence. A grizzled old bastard of a man named Syrus was once found with another farmer's plow oxen. Syrus said the oxen were his and had been for years. There was some debate in the town square where the farmer made the accusations. Some pushing and shoving ensued, but not much more. Syrus was known for his harshness. Children were afraid of him; He was generally a mean fuck with a massive slow-witted son. His wife had died many years before. "Why would I steal yours when I can barely get my fields tilled with just me and my dim son?" He added, "When would I have stolen it? How could I have walked it ten miles along the roads without being seen?"

ON and ON

Syrus then placed a few choice curse words towards his accuser as tobacco juice ran down his stained, gray, tangled beard.

"You are just a selfish, stubborn, dirty fek," his accuser yelled at him. "Nobody likes ye, and ye scare all the women and children!"

"I may be a lot of 'tings, son, but a thief isn't one of them!" Syrus roared back, then added, "And you can go n *fek* yourself!" as he made a humping jester.

A month later, the other farmer burned Syrus and his son in their hut while they slept. Everyone called it justice. I always wondered about the justice served because the arson fella had a bunch of new livestock later that year. My formulated guess is that Syrus, the mean, nasty, socially awkward fuck that he was, had some savings stashed away, and the public announcement of theft was just a calculated plan to steal his shit. That was two thousand years ago. (The statute of limitations has long expired.)

People were ruthless and greedy in every generation. (Human nature.) There were rumors of a woman who would seduce drunk men and rob them after she got them back to her room. The bigger rumor was that the woman was a tiny, feminine man. I don't recall any victim ever admitting someone with a dick seduced them. The Kink's song "Lola" pops into my head whenever I tell that story. If you don't know it, look it up. It's worth your time was just that, life. I'm amazed at how my ignorance was a blessing. Simple life, simple problems.

Everything changed once the Romans arrived. It was not a simple squabble between clans. We are talking about a war machine! Professional soldiers, but more than soldiers. They marched slowly towards us. I remember seeing columns of troops miles long, further than I could see. A few men rode in and met with our leaders. After the meeting, nothing happened. For weeks, the Romans did not launch an attack against us. Life was normal; as usual, I'd plow with my brother Jareth, harvest, and argue with Dad. Jareth would always shake his head at me and say something like, "Why do you always say shit to antagonize him? You know he's right, and you will eventually do it his way." I'd reply with nonsense like, "He could ask instead of demand." I'm not much for being told what to do, especially what I'm not allowed to do. (I did, several times, talk to the Dunbar girls.)

What we needed to know was that the Romans were building fortifications. Word spread of the Romans building a new city. Maybe they just wanted to be neighbors. (Yeah, right.) The speed with which they worked and the dimensions of this new area were unbelievable. Not only were the Romans a wrecking ball of incredible force, but also a class of master craftsmen. I heard some men in town predicting, "I hear they are bringing a thousand women with them." (Men? Seriously, we can't hold more than two thoughts in our heads without reverting to somehow getting laid.) We had no fucking idea of the power they would unleash on us.

Of course, the news arrived well before the army. Being proud, we would not pay tribute to a foreign power nor bend a knee to anyone without a fight. Our counsel told us the Romans wanted complete surrender, no terms or land. They asked for our surrender or to be destroyed. Everyone knew how the invaders would treat us if we lost. No one was eager to be anyone's subject. We were relatively free, but I knew we couldn't defeat them. Thousands of my neighbors and fellow citizens decided to put away our differences; several different clans who hated each other lined up together to face the most powerful army assembled. We had no choice but to fight or surrender. The Romans had blocked us in with their city-like fortifications. No trade was allowed in or out of our town. We were being long-term starved. It might take a year to accomplish their goal, but the longer we held out, the weaker we would be. Eventually, the Romans got tired of waiting moved into position and forced our hand. In my mind, there was no other option but to fight. (We were so fucked!)

I sweated through my light wool shirt the day we lined up across the pass from the Romans. The sun pointed his fingers directly into my eyes. Metal from my enemy's armor blinked like twinkling stars across the field. I watched as the clear sky filled with a dark mist of arrows that rained down upon us, making the sound of a teapot whistling. Thousands of arrows thudded into the ground ten feet before us, announcing the Romans' arrival before we started our charge. Two uncles and three cousins, almost every man in our family, gathered together on that day. My father and I stood side by side; we were more united in our soon-to-be deaths than we ever were in our daily lives. (Strange how it works.) We had left Jareth to watch over the family. He was perfectly capable of handling everything if we did not return. "Far better than you." My father had said this to me the night before. What he was essentially saying was that I was expendable. I guess he was too. But he surprised me, took off his ring that symbolized our family's long lineage, and gave it to me.

"I should have given this to you years ago; I never felt you were ready. You can run now; slip away. We will both die here today. There is no need for it. You are strong and can lead our family. Go!" He said as he charged forward without me.

Fucking, really?" I remember saying to no one but myself. I couldn't run away. He should have given that damn ring to Jareth before we left. Why would that dick put me in this situation? I knew I wasn't running away. Jareth would have to find my body if I didn't make it and pull this stupid ring off my cold finger.

Tens of thousands of my countrymen waited together in near silence. The only voices were some men praying out loud. I looked out before me and counted the arrows sticking from the ground. I was scared but not in a panic. I was determined to rid our land of these unwanted guests. The Roman archers did little to dissuade our resolve. That courage changed quickly when the Roman cavalry charged. Hundreds of simple farmers returned to their homes as the horsemen engaged our army. They rolled through men and crushed them under hoofs and swords. The battle moved in slow motion as I fought hand to hand in a huge mixing bowl of men and blood. We fought for what felt like hours but were probably minutes. My rage was unleashed; I held nothing back for the first time in my life. I had no training but smashed and stabbed wildly, and soon I was exhausted. I had a general feeling that we were losing, and then I felt the long blade enter through my lower back in an upward motion and exited just below my left nipple, severing my heart along the way. I tried to catch my breath and heard my racing heartbeat in my ears as it slowly stopped beating. Then nothing, no white light, no flash of memories, just darkness and a cold damn nothingness.

ON and ON

I'm not saying there isn't an afterlife. I do believe people who have had near-death experiences. I also believe a true god does exist because, obviously, I'm still here. I've also seen some wicked voodoo shit, unexplainable lights in the sky, pyramids thousands of miles apart that look very similar with no possible way for their builders to be connected, healers, Nostradamus's predictions, and people who can communicate with the dead. Yes, I'm a bit of a conspiracy theorist, but if I've learned anything on this journey of mine, it's that anything is possible. I've also had a millennium to ponder such stupid shit. Still, I don't know how everything works. Like, how scientists can predict what another planet looks like, or how the hell block chain works, and the thought of demons and ghosts weirds me the fuck out, but so do needles. What I do know is that I didn't die. Was it the ring my father gave me? I've concluded that it's not the ring, but I haven't taken it off my finger since he gave it to me. It was taken from me twice, but I was able to reclaim it both times.

I was startled awake when a crow landed on my face. It was starting to peck at my right eye. Freaky fucking feeling to wake up with a big-ass evil black bird trying to eat your eye! I fucking hate crows. (But I also hate geese; they are just mean.) One simple head shake didn't dislodge him; I had to grab his leg and pull it off my face. I was scared and disoriented. I immediately grabbed my chest, looking for the bloody wound I had taken. There was no fresh blood, no gaping holes, no pain. There was a hole in my shirt, bottom back, and upper front, but no holes in me. The sword that ran through me had been removed. I had a fresh pink wound on my upper chest, but it was very superficial, and it didn't even really hurt; just kind of a little sore. An hour later, there was no sign I had ever been impaled.

The battle had long since moved on. Bodies were being piled together and burned. I wrapped myself in a dead Roman's cape and walked away. No one stopped me. I kept my head down and walked back towards my family's farm. As I walked, I felt very good physically. Better than ever. An old injury where my right knee had been kicked by our ox several years ago and caused a limp was gone. My vision was better. I heard more clearly. I felt energetic. I was ALIVE! Maybe I had tripped, hit my head, and didn't get stabbed. Whatever had happened, I was walking away from this graveyard and going home! I had to walk slowly to not draw attention to myself, but inside, I was bursting with joy and excitement!

My joy was short-lived. I stopped dead in my tracks the moment I saw the smoke. I knew in my heart where it was coming from. I prayed I was wrong. Rounding the hill to my home, I immediately noticed everything was gone and burned. Every family hut was on fire burning. Our livestock had been killed and butchered in their pens. Every scrap of meat was gone; all that was left was pools of drying blood covered by a black sea of flies. Our small shack of a house was burned to the ground; crisp, glossy wood beams were still smoking. A smokey, pitch-black area was all that was left of where I had lived my entire life. The bodies of my family scorched into burnt logs. I examined the remains of my family's smoldering, blackened shells. They were still almost too hot to touch. One by one, I found the body of every person I loved, each with their throat slit ear to ear. It was evident Jareth had put up a fight; my brother had been sliced diagonally across his entire

ON and ON

body, his wounds making a cooked puffy X, and his head was barely attached. My dear, sweet wife lay in the scarred outline where our house once stood in the spot where our bed was once placed. I know what had happened to her before her death. Two thousand years later, it still sickens and saddens me that I didn't take the time to hide her, one of my many regrets. I had lost everything; nothing was left. No family, no home, no safety. Only the clothes on my back. I couldn't stay but did not know where to go. There wasn't a nearby family friend to take me in; everyone had been killed. Our village was destroyed. I was alone.

Why was I still alive? Was I alive? Could others even see me? Was I a spirit or some ghost? Was I in purgatory? I was too afraid to be seen. The truth of my actual existence had to stay hidden. I couldn't just walk up to our invaders and ask if they could see me. So, like a coward with no revenge in me, I walked away. I had a hole in my heart, both emotionally and literally.

So, I walked. I walked for years without purpose. A lot like Forrest Gump when he ran across America. Except for a darker, sadder story without redemption or a cool soundtrack. I stole, cursed God, begged, tried to drink myself to death, never stayed in one place, was seen as little as possible, and permanently moved along to the next place without purpose. I was always moving away from my homeland, with only one question in my soul. *Why?*

I am still trying to figure out the answer. I have come to realize that there is no honest answer. It's just me, alone, living forever waiting for something. (Who fucking knows what that something is?) I'm here and have been living day to day longer than I can remember. With each day, year, one century, rolling into the next. Years with small eventful experiences mixed in to help me forget just how lonely I am.

ON and ON

Truth? Lies? You decide

I made several attempts to kill myself during those first years. I can't remember how many ways I tried to do it. (It was a lot.) Hanging didn't work; it just hurt. Starvation was just too slow. I'd cut my wrists only to pass out and wake up with healing marks that were gone by lunchtime. I was so distraught that one day, I jumped from a cliff onto jagged rocks, only to awaken with broken legs and a nasty headache. Those injuries healed in less than twelve hours. Serious crazy shit. Unbelievable, actually. Laying on those rocks that day, I decided to live.

Stop feeling sorry for myself. There must be a reason. I had to find it. I was going to start fresh, possibly fall in love, maybe chase wealth, and even help the unfortunate. (Big ideas.) I had no real plan, but I had been given some kind of gift for living, and I was done trying to hurt myself. I would continue my self-deprivation but in more subconscious ways. It's like a stripper getting back at Daddy because she didn't get the love she needed. I became a habitual dick stepper. Which means every time something good was happening, I would find a way to fuck it up. Not purposely, but indeed, the same result. As time passed, I realized that the world was continually stepping on my dick.

I've always been a positive person. (Most times positively an asshole.) I had to reinvent myself from a simple farmer, now irrelevant vagrant, into someone with a purpose for living. I also made a considerable effort not to be angry. (Very difficult!) I wanted to be a different person. I decided that I wasn't as bright as I thought I was. (Handsome and funny, of course.) I wanted to learn new things. I wanted to speak different languages. I wanted to be able to read and write. I wanted to have a better understanding of the world I live in and how things work. That transformation wasn't easy, and it took decades, damn near a hundred years, before I even had a clue. I want to say I was like David Carradine in the 80's TV show *Kung-Fu.* I wanted to roam the countryside, solve crimes, and help people. I love that show, but I'm not nearly that moral or cool. (As you will learn, I watch a lot of TV.)

After deciding to stop hurting myself, I was able to live a series of short lives. Twenty to thirty-year cycles. I could pack in many years of living into those three decades. Some cycles were great; some were lonely as fuck. I'd try different occupations, change locations, and even reinvent my identity. Nothing was off the table. Beach bum to suit and tie office worker (not many of those.) I began to develop habits I could usually break once I realized they were becoming destructive. Early in my life, my worst habit was being mean to everyone. Later in life, I would sometimes overspend to impress people. I could give a fuck less about what they thought of me. I have been a procrastinator. (Duh, I have all the time in the world.) I tried smoking, but it never agreed with me. I would find myself cracking knuckles or repeating the same phrases. I once knew a man who would begin each sentence with, "To be honest or to tell the truth." Then, he would proceed with his statement as if no one would believe his story unless he made it clear that it was truthful. Another friend would always repeat the same statement in the same sentence. "I saw the most beautiful woman this morning, just this morning." Most sailors I knew would use curse words to fill in blanks that didn't need filling in. My father's habit was to rub his chin while pondering the world's truth. In deep thought, he would rub his chin like it held a genie that would grant him three wishes.

The one habit I have kept for all these years is turning that damn ring my father gave me around and around, using my thumb to make circles slowly. I would catch myself staring at it as it slowly made its three-hundred-and-sixty-degree journey around my right ring finger. I was contemplating its value, its meaning, its truth. I didn't dare take it off. Even in times of depression, I wasn't sure if the ring gave me the ability to regenerate every day.

I did some research about the ring itself. It is made of a shiny metal. It's not gold or silver. It's a very rare metal; I have yet been able to identify what exactly it is made from. Maybe a meteorite. No one knows. It has a small emerald stone in the center and a three-point enclosed spiral design. It was almost as if three minor quotation marks came together. I learned that the type of ring is a *Triskelion*, also called a triple cycle.

Derived from the Greek word "Triskeles," meaning "three legs," the Triskele or Triple Spiral is a complex ancient Celtic symbol. Often referred to by many as a Triskelion, its earliest creation dates back to the Neolithic era.

Each point represents either the holy trinity or the spirit of the mind, body, and soul. Depending on the book or expert. I have talked to many historians, and all have a different interpretation of what exactly my nemesis ring represents. One jeweler told me it was a cheap knockoff made in China. Someone told me it was very rare and I would consider selling it. Since I knew it was not from China and would never sell it, they were both of little help. So it's just the fucked up ring my father gave me at the worst possible time to encourage my cowardness that could possibly hold the key to immortality. (Or a cheap Chinese knockoff.)

The ring is a part of me, almost like an extra finger, so often I forget it's even on my finger.

ON and ON

<u>Death on a horse</u>

I returned to America after a few hundred-year sabbatical. I found myself playing poker in a dusty ass Midwestern plains town (upper Texas panhandle area.) The plains are a wondrous sight. Brown, dry grass, as far as you can see. There are no mountains, just a light brown ocean of small dirty trees and hills that roll on like the moon pulling the ocean current. Sitting at a table with those rangers I spoke of earlier who were chasing Comanche Indians. I was bored with life. I needed something to get me out of a yearlong depression. I decided what I needed was an adventure. I specifically traveled to the plains because it was the wildest murderous region in the world at the time (just before the American Civil War.) White pioneers sought a better life, and the American government passed out free land. Problematic because groups of native people already owned that same land. Several Indian tribes already called it home. Tribes had lived in this hot as fuck, environment with very little water, grass/desert region for centuries. Interesting footnote: The Spanish conquistadors had tried to take these same lands after wiping out the Aztec Empire and failed miserably. Native American tribes just kicked the shit out of those Spanish bastards. The Spanish were not prepared for the harshness of the climate, the terrain, and especially the savagery enforced upon them by warriors on horseback. I've always found it interesting that such a small force of Spanish conquistadors could decimate the Aztec empire but could never even hold a settlement in Comanche territory.

Comanche Native American Indians were a nation of fearsome fighters. They were remarkably similar to the Spartans warrior class civilization. Grown and taught to ride horseback and deliver death. The Comanche culture was linked to torture and death, with some thievery mixed in. (They also loved to gamble.) They were expert horsemen and skilled archers with a desire to rob and mutilate any enemy regardless of sex or age. To put it very simply, these were the baddest motherfuckers on the planet. I had to see them. What I did eventually see was far more heart-stopping than I ever expected.

I had some previous experience with men who called themselves Texas Rangers, so I fully understood that Texas Rangers are either very competent warriors or complete lunatic backward-ass dumb fucks. I say this because damn near anyone could claim to be a Ranger. There was usually no pay. They didn't receive a tin star to pin on their vest like in the movies. Mostly it was young men who had just left momma's tit and were looking to make a name for themselves. Men who didn't want to work but wanted an excuse to kill Indians. My new friends were not those idiots. They were ex-military, and they were hilarious, raucous, full of shit, and full of themselves. I loved them immediately. Small talk at a poker table turned into a quick friendship. I remember the meaner looking of them, Sawyer saying to me, "Damn, son, you must be the palest man in all of Texas."

"But that lucky card caching sumbitch can drink," added Dusty.

(They reminded me of the *Lonesome Dove* Rangers in Larry McMurtry's novel, except they were both Gus.) By the end of the first night, we were old friends. We talked shit to each other. They referred to me as cocksure. (I later found out that it meant cocky.) They nicknamed me Fiery, but it sounded more like Furry when they said it.

ON and ON

Sawyer had sort of a "resting bitch face," but instead of bitch face, it was a resting fuck you up face. He just looked mean. Sometimes, he would pause between comments, and that small moment would make you feel incredibly uncomfortable and possibly expect that he would come unglued and attack you. Then he would say something outrageous like, "Furry, you cocksure sumbitch, I'm playin' even money I could hog tie you in lesson bout thirty seconds." then he added, "I ain't gonna do it, you're too funny, everyone here likes your company."

I'm guessing that was his way of telling me I was close to getting my ass beat. It was a rhetorical statement, one without a response requirement. So, I just looked him in the eyes and smiled. (He did not smile back.) Sawyer was very average-looking, almost forgettable. His stone-cold killer stare was not. His eyes were just a smidge too close together. He was like a rattlesnake; you want to look at it but from a long distance away.

Dusty was a string bean. He was what Sawyer called "wirrry." He always had a smile on his face. The crinkles around his eyes did not smile. He was aware of every movement and every person's placement and had a quick, funny reply ready at any moment. Nothing was off limits between them. I heard them say mean, hurtful shit to each other that was retorted with something worse. For no other reason than they hadn't said something terrible to each other in five minutes, Sawyer tosses a verbal volley.

"Hey Dust, your momma still riding every man's pole in East Texas?"

Immediately, Dusty shot back, "You still mad because she didn't want your little twig? You shouldn't hold on to things, Saw, it just ain't healthy, is that why your face is hard to look at, is that why you's always look so damned angry?"

Continually back and forth between them. It was best to stay out of their way. Otherwise, they'd both gang up on you. I learned that lesson the hard way. I threw a quick jab in while they were in the middle of one of their exchanges.

"You two are like brothers who haven't figured out who the alpha dog is." I mistakenly and unwantedly butted in. I saw them both pause and look at me, both with a Who-the-fuck-does-this-guy-think-he-is? look on their faces. I decided to make a quick exit outside to take a piss. They followed me out and waited for a moment, then began to pummel me verbally.

"You know that's illegal west of the Mississippi, son?" Dusty said to me.

"What's that?" I replied, midstream, not looking at them.

"Grown man holding a little boy's pecker." Sawyer laughed.

I'd never heard that one before, and it made me laugh so hard that I peed a little on my pants. Luckily, they were too busy slapping each other on the back to notice, and I turned and walked back into the saloon.

I'm positive I had been cheated a few times but could give a fuck less. I did make a stand once when Dusty tried to claim that a four-card straight beat my two pairs. (It doesn't.)

ON and ON

"I don't know how ya'll play wherever the fuck your Furry ass comes from, but here in Texas, a straight is a straight." Dusty tried to explain.

"Nowhere does a four-card straight beat anything. Not even in the great Lone Star territories. That *is* a great lowball hand." I volleyed back to him. (Lowball is a poker game where the worst hand wins) "You boys out here play a lot of lowball with life," I added.

He sat quietly for a second, then pushed the money my way. Of course, he couldn't be outdone and said, "You have no fucking idea!" with his smiling face and unsmiling eyes.

When they had enough of my money and whiskey for the night, they invited me along for their current assignment, a chase they thought would last just a few weeks. So, of course, I had to tag along. Fortunately, most people generally find my company appealing. I have an easy demeanor that flows effortlessly with most people.

These guys reminded me of a type of knight's guard. I want to say, without the arrogance, that these guys were *humbly arrogant*, if that makes any sense. They carried themselves with confidence and spoke slowly in a matter-of-fact way. They gave off a "don't *fuck with us aura*" in a hospitable way. They were very nice, polite badasses with huge Colt 45 pistols strapped to their hips. I am drawn to conflict and fun, too. (Actually, more drawn to fun, drinking, and stupid shit, but also conflict. I did tell you I can't die. And I heal quickly?) Why wouldn't I be drawn to conflict? Over the years, I found quite a bit of conflict (and fun).

I helped them track and chase for about twenty days. I was generally very little help. Instead, I rode and drank with those boys every day, is what I did. They taught me to be a better shot with a pistol (those Colt revolvers were an amazing new technology.) How to better read a tracking trail and a lot about the Comanches. I had heard stories and read a few dime store novels about these Indians and what a Comanche could do on a horse. The truth wasn't close to my expectations about their horsemanship or savagery.

I enjoyed my days on the open plains. The Texas sun was hot, but the weather could change instantly. One morning I awoke to seeing my breath and barely feeling my toes. In an hour, I was bare-chested, looking at a potential sunburn. Only to quickly take shelter from a monsoon rainstorm that lasted only ten minutes but created a muddy bog that added ten pounds of mud to my boots. That night, under a full moon, I learned some new drinking songs, like "There's a skeeter on my Peter" and a version of a song about "checking your woman for ticks." Lots of fun drunk times.

During the day, however, it was all tracking business. From sunrise to sundown, they had a job to do. We also had one long night ride with the help of a full moon. The thing I found most interesting was that those rangers had respect for the men they chased. The little tricks used to throw us off the trail fascinated them, and they spent hours discussing every detail.

"Now, how in *the* hell do six horses just disappear and magically reappear yonder over there?"

"Even stranger, how does that light-skinned furry fella fry in the sun all day and not get baked like pork cracklins?" was Sawyers' reply. While he stared at me. I just smiled and turned my horse to follow the

ON and ON

rest of the men, leaving Dusty and Sawyer to discuss the tracking amongst themselves.

Comanches almost stole our horses one night, and if it were not for one of the men taking a midnight leak, they would have been successful. In Comanche culture, the ownership of horses was significant, but the stealing of horses, "the story of how they obtained the horses," was the telling of who you were as a Comanche. If they had succeeded in stealing our horses, that Comanche would have gained status, and we would have been fucked. (We were at least a hundred miles from the closest fort and with very little water.) Neither Ranger bad-mouthed those renegades.

On the contrary, I only heard them speak about their intelligence, how even adolescent Indians knew more about how to live off the land than they ever would. Dusty and Sawyer always bounced several ideas between each other. I remember one story about a rite of passage that all Comanche boys must endure to be considered a man. Boys aged between ten and twelve left camp alone and could only return with claws and skins from a mountain lion. It was a common legend that was generally believed to be accurate. Men from the Rangers group added bits of color to the story to include boys who never returned, boys who were found mutilated, and boys who were captured. All of this was always just hearsay. All the men knew a common story about a Comanche named Running Moon. He returned to camp just three days after leaving. A mountain lion had eaten half of his backside. The story says he encountered the mountain lion the first night he left. He didn't attack it; it attacked him in his sleep. Running Moon was rendered unconscious, and the lion began to dine on him. He was able to fight it off and returned to camp where he was labeled as a coward and banished; his remains were left just a mile outside of the village.

Every night, there were several stories told. The best story I heard was about Quanah Parker. His saga had been romanticized for generations. Like all boys starting their journey, he left camp with only the clothes on his back and a buffalo bladder filled with water. Parker returned two years later; he had been assumed dead. When he returned, he wore the skins of several mountain lions. His face was disfigured by three deep scars that ran diagonally from his hairline to under his chin. His breastplate was decorated with the claws of twenty lions. His return included more than one hundred stolen horses, a multitude of enslaved people, and six wives. Parker's story is even more incredible because he was half-white. His mother was Cynthia Ann Parker, a white pioneer woman kidnapped as a small child. Cynthia was raised Comanche and eventually married a man of high tribal standing. The tales of Quanah Parker's bravery during his youth transformation journey are told repeatedly at every campfire in the Midwest plains. Killing his first mountain lion with just a knife and receiving his life-long facial scars in return was a favorite. Tracking an older male for weeks to finally take pity on the beast and let it escape is an example of his softer side. Some tells are unbelievable, such as hiding in a beaver lodge, underwater, breathing through a reed to pounce on a lion while it is drinking, or disguising himself in a buffalo hide to lasso a fierce female and take her as his pet. (One of my personal favorites.)

His real history may not be as impressive as the tall tells, but he did accomplish unifying a group of people who had never been united in their history. Quanah Parker brings his people together to unite against

ON and ON

anyone and everyone trying to live or even travel in their lands. He organizes raids against settlers and army forts from Oklahoma, through Texas, and deep into Mexico. He is believed to be the youngest and longest-standing Comanche chief ever. He was instrumental in negotiations with the American government, helping establish a Comanche reservation in Oklahoma. (I love the side note history lessons.)

Stories like this were told and retold during my time with the Rangers. A new tidbit of information or fable was always tossed in to increase the tall tells value, but at the end of the night, it always came back to Dusty and Sawyer fucking with each other.

"I don't know about ya'll, but after a month or so, I need a comfy bed and a warm woman." Dusty proclaimed one night.

"If in I was of mind; I hear those red ladies can make you forget all about a soft bed." Sawyer couldn't resist to add.

"If in you were of mind? Who you trin to bamboozle? I seen some of those large hairy arm-pitted women you paid for in Laredo; you'd stick your willy in anything that have you?"

One early morning on the twentieth day, we found a trail and quietly tracked it to a band of about a dozen young braves. Looking back, I remember thinking to myself, it's odd for them to be so unaware and not on guard. I wasn't in charge, and it wasn't my place to voice my opinions. They were relaxing by their campfire as if they didn't have a care in the world. We stormed in, bullets flying. Our prey quickly mounted their ponies and high-tailed it around a slight bend in the river. We crested the bend, hell-bent on catching up. I've since learned what happens next is the equivalent of the Indian version of the *oldest trick in the book*. A fucked-up rookie mistake. (I would not have expected Sawyer and Dusty to fall for it.) Waiting for us around that corner were the Indians we had been tracking. A 200-plus war-painted, death-on-horseback Comanche war party. The dozen adolescents were bait, and we took it hook, line, and sinker. As did many soldiers in the coming years. To the Ranger's credit, our band of thirty men didn't run and hide. The last words I remember from Dusty were, "Well Fuck!"

These brave Texas Rangers, full of pride and honor, charged full speed in with guns blazing. Several painted warriors fell dead off their horses immediately. I know I got at least one. We were quickly surrounded and rounded up into a kind of fish bait ball-shaped formation, like how dolphins maneuver anchovies close together. They moved into a multi-circular wheel rotating in opposite directions. I remember being utterly amazed and scared as shit at the same time. (In this situation, I felt death was finally going to happen!) We didn't stand a snowball's chance in hell. I had never nor have I ever since witnessed horsemanship anywhere close to what I saw that day.

No saddles. They were riding at full speed and shooting arrows quickly and accurately. I saw them use their horses as shields and continue to shoot arrows from under their horses' necks. Were they holding on by maybe a heel? I don't know how they did what they did. I'd love to say we rode straight through them, bringing carnage from every pistol, but the truth is I took a total of fourteen arrows placed in every section of my body. I remember every fucking one of them, including the five that were shot into me after I was unsaddled and lying in the dirt, drooling dark blood-ridden saliva from my mouth. Needless to say,

ON and ON

that shit fucking hurt. It *really* hurt. I got a first-hand reenactment of how those conquistadors met their fate. I did not witness my ranger friends' deaths. I awoke sometime later to a horrific scene of blood, death, and blatant torture. Every man in our group was dead. Half looked like porcupines with over fifty arrows sticking out of them in every direction.

Several others were mutilated beyond recognition. And let's say there are some things I won't mention nor want to remember. Everyone, including myself, had been scalped. (I was so happy; I was unconscious and don't have that painful memory.) Pushing and pulling those arrows out wasn't pleasant. Oh, and they took all our horses too. It was the worst ass-kicking I ever took. My wounds healed, and my scalp grew back by the following day. I learned that not having water for two weeks won't kill me either. I walked fucking forever back to civilization, got on a boat, and got the fuck outta Texas. I realized I should not be so arrogantly eager to seek danger. What did I think was going to happen? These savages were going to invite me into their society? My pale Celtic ass was going to join a buffalo hunt like Kevin Costner in *Dances with Wolves*? Court, all their women? Fucking stupid! But lesson learned.

<u>Pote</u>

About six hundred years earlier, I found myself on the shores of the Mediterranean Sea. Crew members were needed for the many ships sailing the new trade routes. I had just outgrown my family, literally. I looked so much younger than my 45-year-old wife, and my youthfulness would only cause trouble. I had to leave and make it look like I was dead. One day, I came home and told her of an argument with a stranger in a tavern in a nearby town. I pretended to rage, saying, "I can't let him get away speaking to me as if I'm a peasant. I'm going to go back and teach that bastard a lesson." (Or some bullshit like that.)

I left her financially secure for a few generations. Leaving someone you love is never easy, but I couldn't stay. I had been putting off leaving for about five years, and it was time. It makes me sad to think of the many times I have selfishly abandoned someone I loved. I will be alone for over a hundred years, then find a woman to love for twenty years, then alone again. Back and forth forever, it seems. I fooled myself into thinking that leaving her financially secure made up for disappearing. (It didn't.) It sucked, but I had to leave.

I was eager to find something new. Penniless again, I was left with only the clothes on my back. I found a berth on an old wreck of a barge called the *Troyana*. I didn't know much about ships at the time. It looked like a wreck, and I wondered if it would float out of the harbor. She was a dark sea-battered brown. Every board looked waterlogged, like a balloon ready to burst. A light white salty ring wrapped around her just above the water level. Huge poles stretched upward, holding spectacular cream-colored sails. Looking at her, I wasn't entirely sure I wanted to take a ride, but since I hadn't tried drowning or being eaten by a sea monster, I said, ' Why the fuck not?" I inquired about joining the crew. It was my first encounter with Captain Quinones. My first impression was that he was an uppity arrogant, privileged paper pusher, probably using Daddy's money to increase his stature. He was exactly who I expected to be running the show. He was tall and very thin. Dressed as if attending a ceremony to receive a merit badge. He wore a long ponytail that pulled his hairline back to the middle of his skull. "This is a year-long adventure traversing the Atlantic Ocean." he continued to speak, but the foul odor passing from his lips almost made me puke. I didn't hear another word he spoke. I tried to ease back away from him, but he closed the gap. My eyes started to water. I held my breath. He said something, then something else, until I finally heard, "......we have a position as a cook."

With no experience, I was happy to accept the as a cook. It was either cooking or being a cabin boy. I was way too old and heterosexual to be a cabin boy, so cook it was. I overcame seasickness every morning, but it soon returned; this repeated for a few days. Until I got what was referred to as "my sea legs." My cooking skills sharpened after a week, or at least no one complained anymore. I learned the language of the sea. Starboard from the port. Bow from the stern. Helm, jib, heeling, lines, booms, and many more. I made friends with most of the crew. Many were poor men trying to earn a wage. Some were criminals escaping the gallows. Others were men trying to advance their stature in life.

I did not give trust easily, but months at sea with no land in sight brought forth trust and love for most of my fellow sailors. The crew immediately called me Pote e leche, which translates precisely to *a can of milk*. Then, eventually, it just became Pote, for short. Why can and not milk? No fucking idea. That shit just stuck. Pote, that's me, I guess, the white can of milk. It could have been way worse. Another crew member was called shit bird or *la mierda Pajaro*. I don't know what a shit bird looks like, but if I ever did see a shit bird, I'm positive it would look just like him.

No crew member was a simple Spaniard or Italian. Everyone was a mixed breed. I happen to be the fairest of them all. Luckily, they didn't dub me Snow White. (I know it wasn't a story yet.) Because I was white-ish and new, the crew played practical jokes on me, like gluing my boots to the deck or being put on anchor watch. I was eventually able to win them over by threatening, "I'll just add cow shit to the stew."

I did give them all a nice case of the runs after the five-hour anchor watch detail. I watched them eat and smiled at them, and suddenly the jokes stopped. (I only threatened.) I did much more than cook; I learned to sail. I learned knot tying, new curse words, and all the jobs on a ship sailing the ocean. I learned how to read the stars for navigation. I also learned who not to fuck with, and his name was first mate David Palos. Mr. Palos was a solid guy, a terrible card player, had a pleasant singing voice, knew many dirty songs, was an excellent sailor, and was not much for taking shit from anyone not named Captain Quinones. "Da-vid," as he was called, knew the captain was not up to the task of handling the men on our ship, so he did. I saw him

ON and ON

beat the shit out of a swabby who said something to the effect of, "I'll decide when I work; you can fuck off for now." That guy looked like a badass, too. Palos made it look effortless. I tried to be Palos' friend or at least drinking buddy. I ended up being both. David Palos was not a large man. He didn't cast a huge shadow; he was fighting lean.

All muscle and sinew. A premature balding head and a crooked nose and smile. I never saw him yawn; he was always freshly shaved, no matter the time of day or night. Professional sailor. He mainly was business but liked a few cups of rum after dark. He was the one who gave me most of my sailing knowledge. I was eager to learn; he knew of my inexperience and took it as his job to explain the ways of the seas to me. He once told me, "There is something different about you. You're much smarter than all these peasants. You listen. You learn quickly. And you work hard. How and why are you here on this boat?"

I said, "I wanted to see the world."

He just nodded his head as if he understood completely. "I wanted to sail the moment I saw the ocean for the first time. It never frightened me, only invited me in for more," he answered. I'm not sure if he was talking to me or himself.

Most people's idea of a crew's appearance back then is probably based on a movie or book you experienced. This crew was a bit of both; some were ragtag, as you would imagine, but others were professional sailors, young apprentices, and old-time soldiers. Personal conflicts did happen between the crew. Some were as simple as someone getting a bigger portion at dinner, and other times as severe as theft. A personal item of no material value but dearly valuable to the owner would be taken from a bunk occasionally. We didn't have lockers or master locks, so you either kept your personal effects on your person or left them where you slept. This one time, funny enough, I recall exactly what was taken. Men kept all sorts of meaningless shit. From trinkets that a whore gave them to bird bones. (People have bizarre superstitions.) One guy had the rattles from a huge rattlesnake that he found. He carried those rattles everywhere. He just liked the rattling sound.

Patty Boy was a large, very agile Italian. He had the bushiest eyebrows and the calmest demeanor. He exploded into a red rage when he could not find an item his mom had given to him.

"WHO took it!" Pat screamed in Italian. "I'll crush your bones into a paste, you dirty mother fucker!"

Most men could not understand him; he was obviously livid, but why? No one had seen this side of the hairy beast.

"Someone stole something of his," I explained to everyone.

"Who took what?" someone yelled.

I shrugged my shoulders and looked at Big Patty Boy for the answer.

"My comb!" he cried.

That brought a chorus of laughter from the entire ship. Patty Boy was skin scalp bald. Not even a little peach fuzz. The crew's raucous laughter drew out more rage, and he almost had to be restrained. The man responsible was easy to locate. He was the only crew member with a freshly combed mane. (Stupid fuck!) That comb was Patty's only item from his mother, a woman he deeply cherished.

ON and ON

Palos sided with Patty Boy and beat the living shit out of the man with the newly detangled hair; he looked a lot like Dee Snider from Twisted Sister (a late 1980s hair band.) Palos put him on limited rations for a week. The best part of this story is that Patty Boy shared some of his meals with him. (As I said earlier, I've seen crazy shit.)

Speaking of shit, we sailed with a cargo of grape seed and cattle. The smell was unbearable. Our poor cabin boy Diego and another man whom, I can't remember his name, had to look after them. Terrible job. We got fresh milk daily and butchered a few steers for meat. The plan was to sail to an island chain called the Azores off of the African coast and trade the cattle for gold, then sail to Rio De Janeiro and buy slaves to be sold in the Caribbean. Slaves were needed for sugar and rum production. I was just the cook and had no idea we would be slavers. (Nobody asked me for a moral opinion.)

The first leg of the trip was uneventful. After two months of nothing but wind and stars, we had a week-long stay in the Azores. The waters surrounding the island chain were as blue-green as peacock feathers mixed with robin eggs. In deeper water, the ocean turned into a smashed blueberry stain. Beautiful but uninviting. Beaches with sand as black as a black widow's back surrounded most islands. Blacker than the devil's heart. Multi-colored fish swam everywhere. So many new things to see and do. I was bursting with excitement to get off the ship. It was a world I had no idea existed.

To say that we partied was a colossal understatement. No rules, some coins in our pockets, and everything for sale? (Use your imagination, it was awesome!) The island was paradise. Dolphins playing in the surf. Birds of every possible color pattern that none of us had seen before were everywhere. My most significant discovery was sea turtles! WTF!!! Giant ass turtles I had never heard of coming onto the beach and laying eggs in the sand. It was make-believe. No one I told in Europe years later believed me. (I would not have believed me.) The natives killed and ate some of those turtles, but only a few of the hundreds that lived on the islands. The turtle soup was decent, but I didn't love it. They made weapons and jewelry from the shell. I wore a turquoise turtle shell necklace for years after that day: Sun, sand, and rum for eight full days.

There were also geothermal hot springs. I soaked in those tubs for hours. After we were all louse-free, keeping parasite-free was a real challenge. We set sail from the Azores with a new camaraderie and high morale. Wait, I almost forgot. We ate ice cream. That may sound simple, but it was like nothing we had ever tasted. Santa Maria island is now world-renowned for its ice cream; we supplied the milk cows for the start-up. I got my first brain freeze. It is also known for its cattle breeding, meat production, and wine. I helped start all that shit, too; pretty fucking cool!

Things didn't go as smoothly on the next leg of the journey. Quinones was a dick. He became an arrogant, self-righteous uptight asshole. He made everything happening on the ship his business. (Which I guess it was.) The foul-smelling cows were gone, but he smelled worse. He became a micro-manager about shit he didn't understand. There was serious talk of mutiny. Just a mention of that word was cause to be tossed overboard. I just listened to the rumors and didn't say shit! Two of the former criminal crewmates hatched a plan to kill Quinones and take the gold from the cattle sale. Killing him and stealing the gold was doable. The problem was, then, what? They couldn't hide on the ship. There was nowhere to put the gold. A more significant issue would be the loyalty of the first mate, Mr. Dave Palos. Their plan was simple enough: get Palos drunk, subdue him, and kill the captain. Simple. Except, those two dumbasses talked too much. Pretty soon, everyone on the ship knew what they were planning. I didn't have anything against those two, and killing the captain wasn't a terrible idea, but fucking with Palos was a no-go for me.

I mentioned earlier that I would tell you about the great men history never knew. Palos was one of them and is very high on my list. He was a badass from low-class poverty, leaving home as a child and getting his first job on a ship at seven years old to work his way to become a first mate, which was damn near impossible at this time in history. Low-borns did not rise into managerial roles. He would sometimes share stories from his youth. Similar situations exist with millions of kids across generations and continents. Not enough money, which caused domestic problems. Drunk asshole, dad. He never felt like he belonged anywhere but on a ship, sailing the world's oceans. His difference was a desire to one day be a captain of his ship. It wasn't just a far-off dream. He was working to make it happen. He already had an excellent reputation; he had sailed for over twenty years with a stellar record. Stories were told at night about some of the amazing shit Palos had seen and done. Pirate attacks, ships shooting cannonballs at each other, and shipwreck stories were all associated with Palos. He would wave a couple of fingers in a "wasn't that big of a deal" motion. Never a denial but never an "I did that shit," either. It only added to his street (ocean) cred! He had some gruesome burn scars on the back of his head and neck that proved he was somewhere when something terrible happened. Captain Quinones's father personally chose him for this voyage with a promise of a berth of his own upon successful return.

Palos had become my mentor, and there was no way I was letting these two degenerates hurt him. Palos didn't need my help; he had heard the rumors and played along. They picked a night with little moon and put their plan in motion. I could see that Palos was playing along. On previous occasions, I had seen him drink twice the rum he did that night and not show any signs of intoxication. (Slip #1.)

Palos slurred his words, lost balance a few times, and even spoke nonsense about missing his mom. One of the criminals even tried talking shit to Palos to evoke a reaction. (Slip #2.) Both men slipped away while Palos had his eyes closed in apparent drunkenness. Once they left, Palos opened his eyes and followed them without saying a word. I quietly followed also. I could hear them congratulating themselves on their way to the captain's quarters.

"Fuck Palos, I'll slit that drunk fool's throat later tonight." (Their arrogant stupidity still makes me chuckle.)

When they arrived at the captain's quarters, the cabin boy Diego tried to stop them but was quickly bashed in the head and tossed aside. That kid had heart, especially with Quinones treating him like shit daily. Palos waited until they had entered the captain's quarters. I wondered why he waited. Palos didn't need probable cause. He could do whatever he wanted with any suspected mutiny. He could have killed

ON and ON

them on just the rumors alone. My question was answered when the captain began to beg for his life. Seeing the two men enter his room, he fell on the floor, crying, begging, and acting like a total bitch. I saw the smile appear on Palos' face, and then I knew. He had predicted not only the crime and how it was to be carried out but also the cowardness of the captain. It would give him an edge for later use. (I loved that guy!) Palos walked behind the first criminal and quietly slit his throat. The only sound was a low gurgling, just like in the movies. Quinones saw what had happened and instantly changed character. He became defiant and full of courage. "Threaten to kill me?" he yelled at the remaining mutineer.

"I'll have your head for your disrespect!" he laid it on.

Palos asked the Captain if he wanted to take his sword and serve justice himself to the remaining man. (of course, he didn't) Palos slightly turned to me, and I saw the humor in what he had said. The remaining man's name was Jesse, I think. He was a skinny, sneaky, horse-faced man. Seeing Palos (and me, I like to think), he immediately surrendered. He figured he could talk his way out of it. He blamed his dead friend for all of it.

"It wasn't my idea; he forced me into participating. I was only going to warn the good captain." he tried in vain to explain. (All bullshit and slip #3)

Jesse was put in chains below the deck. Palos made an example out of him the following day. He cut several gashes onto him, made sure he was bleeding profusely, made him confess, and tossed his ass overboard. The sharks came immediately. The entire crew was instructed to watch until he finally went under. (Example shown.)

Our captain was an imbecile. A tall sack of bones with a massive beak of a nose. He had the worst hairline and foulest breath I've ever experienced. Those were his best qualities. I swear he was seasick for half the voyage. In hindsight, knowing what I know today, he had an autoimmune disease like Crohn's, maybe Lupus. His temper was like a hair trigger on a gun. Later, this would end up being his demise. He would fly into a fit of spit and curse words that were an unrecognizable hodgepodge of several languages. He was all elbows and dragon breath due to any number of unforeseen events.

"Too much salt.... not enough salt...... no wind..... too much wind......"

It became comical. Too comical. The Captain once caught the young cabin boy Diego smiling during one of his daily blowups and tossed the poor boy overboard. He grabbed him by his waistline and hip-tossed him over the rail. It happened so quickly that I was caught off guard. We were able to throw little Diego a rope and pull him back aboard after we drug him for a couple of hours.

Aside from translating criminal cases, studying for my sailor's bar exam, and providing security details for a man who didn't need protection, I was also the cook. (My only real job.) I provided top-notch gourmet meals prepared in a state-of-the-art cooking facility. My meals always included unseasoned beans, very few vegetables, and questionably rubbery meats. There was a simple system of oats and eggs for breakfast, no lunch, and beans with meat for dinner. On special occasions, I'd throw in some very hard-crusted bread. Cooking

ON and ON

wasn't difficult, but there is an old saying that says, "You can't make chicken salad with chicken shit." Given what I had to use, I had very few options for what I could serve. There wasn't a suggestion box for the crew to make requests. I just had to ensure I rationed what I had to feed everyone until our next port stop. Feeding the crew full rations became much more demanding as the trip progressed, especially considering we had to dump half our load of dry goods while running from an unidentified vessel that our captain, Senor Quinones, assumed carried a "band of ruthless cutthroats who wanted our ship." Nobody wanted our ship. I will say, in a pinch, the *Troyana* could fly.

After outrunning the fishing boat, I mean pirates. Our food ration was cut to very little. An attempted mutiny, an execution, and very low food stocks. The morale was extremely low. First mate Palos convinced Captain Halitosis to detour into a port not far off our route. The island of Georgetown is a disappointing dot of an island, somewhat on our way to Rio de Janeiro. It was nothing like the Azores. No trees. Just rock and sand. The biggest land animal is a crab. Millions of those uneatable little bastards. The island was just a stopover for vessels sailing to the West Indies. It did become a naval base for the British in the early 1800s. (I hope they improved their accommodations.) Very little to do. Not even a stocked tavern. The refilling was to be a stop-and-go. Palos suggested we didn't even get off the ship. The captain thought otherwise, "Let them stretch their legs." (We were all happy to get off that fucking boat.)

We were headed to Rio de Janeiro, the largest slave trading port in the world, where we were to pick up slaves and drop them off in the Caribbean. I'm just going to say it was a different time, and the reality of slavery is horrific but sadly widespread even now. I am only telling a story. I can't change history. (Spoiler alert! The story turns out ok for our cargo in this one.)

Shockingly, while resupplying on Georgetown, our dumb ass captain pissed off one of the local officials. Someone (I forget who) had their honor threatened or was dishonored - got their feelings hurt- and could not stand the insult. My guess is the local fella offered Captain Quinones a breath mint or toothbrush. A duel was suggested, and a good old-fashioned fistfight was offered. Not being the least bit honorable, Quinones sucker punched the local while his back was turned. First mate Palos, being the scrappy SOB he was, came to the jumped-in to fight for our captain. Since the crew loved and feared Palos, we all figured a little melee might be fun. It wasn't.

Captain Quinones escalated the matter by running a saber through the local guy and hightailed it back to the ship. I came to find out the disagreement was about lack of payment. Quinones wanted to give an IOU instead of some of the gold we had on the ship. (Greedy fuck.) Who will provide you with goods just because your daddy is Governor or General of someplace thousands of miles away? So, we stole shit from them with the promise of payment someday if we ever got back this way. It was like three to one against us and not looking good. It was like a bar fight but outside. Men engaged with each other in multiple small boxes. We held off the locals and made it back to the resupplied ship. Unfortunately, first mate Palos had suffered a mortal injury and didn't make it through the night. It's often just like that: there's a fight, your toughest dude takes a hammer to the back of his head, and he dies. It sucked. I've seen many men die, good men die,

ON and ON

but David Palos' death still chokes me up. I wanted to be on the crew of the ship he captained.

A storm, more verbal bullshit, a small breakout of diarrhea, pissing out your ass diarrhea, off course for a couple of days, no real wind to push us, and foul tempers eventually boiled over into full-blown mutiny. Well, not precisely mutiny at first. Remember I told you earlier that that nasty temper would cost Captain Quinones? I won't say it was right, but that dumb, evil-breath, pompous fool of a captain had no business leading a conga dance line. He should have never been in charge of the kind of men who had nothing to lose by joining this crew. He flew into a rage about something I don't even remember what, and Palos wasn't there to stop us. So, we killed the fucker! He wasn't the first man I had murdered, nor the last, but his death does not weigh on my conscience. I haven't lost a second of sleep over him. I only think about him when I'm telling this story or when I catch a whiff of a terrible smell.

We had a few issues to overcome with the captain and first mate dead. First, who was in charge? Secondly, who was going to negotiate the securing of our soon-to-be cargo? We could have divided up the gold from our first stop, made port, and walked away. That was the consensus of most of the crew. A few others saw the bigger picture of turning that small amount of gold into real life-changing money. None of our crew could be called captain material, but someone had to pretend to be a captain, like Donald Sutherland, who was asked to pretend to be a general in the war movie *The Dirty Dozen*.

Eventually, it was decided I would be in charge. I could read and write, a skill I had acquired from a tavern owner's daughter (plus a couple of other skills she taught me) several hundred years ago. I could speak several languages, and I looked the part, well, kind of looked the part. I may have looked too much like a can of milk. In the end, it came down to having all my teeth. The crew decided having teeth was a sign of being highborn.

Now in charge, we set the ship sail to Rio. I thoroughly searched the captain's quarters and found the gold we would need to purchase our new cargo. I also found a case of excellent brandy. (Which I shared a little at a time. The last thing I needed was to be the next captain murdered.)

Surprisingly, we made it to Rio and bought our cargo without problems. It was a straightforward transaction; the old saying "money talks bullshit walks" is true. I'd like to think I made a fine captain. Patty Boy was in charge of the slave purchase; I could not bring myself to do it—we bought one hundred slaves. We would sell them for ten times the price we paid. It was going to be a very lucrative venture.

After we had loaded the cargo, we set sail immediately. That pissed a few of the crew off, but I wanted to get the hell out of there. No need to press our luck. We were scheduled to sail directly to the West Indies. The demand for sugar had exploded worldwide, and workers (free labor) were in high demand. After a half-day on the sea, I was informed that one of our slaves wanted to talk to me. His name was Abskol. He was a large, very dark man. He had intellectual eyes that could burn right through you. He spoke as a man of education. He knew several

ON and ON

languages. He told me, "I should not be enslaved; I am a member of my tribe's royal family. " He was caught up in the round-up because he was somewhere he should not have been. That's right: he was sneaking off to see a woman from the rival tribe. (A few women), he says.

It was easier for strong tribes to capture, enslave, and sell weaker ones. Instead of busting your ass all day in the fields, you and some of the strong men from your village go and get other fools to do the work for you. Human nature. The strong take, and the weak suffer. Someone stronger always existed, and slaveholders could become slaves themselves very quickly. Absko tells me, "My family will pay a handsome reward for my safe return." then adds, "My father is the leader of a mighty and wealthy tribal family."

He also asked, "But it can't be known where I was or what I was doing." (I'm sure they already knew that Absko was led by his dick, but that's just a side note.) The idea of selling humans didn't sit well with me anyway, and if this reward were substantial enough, I wouldn't have to sell anyone.

After discussing the situation with the rest of the crew, we decided to take a chance at Absko's offer. We sailed up the Opara River. Aside from the Amazon, the Opara is the largest river in Brazil. Sailing up the muddy dark water was difficult due to its shallowness and lack of winds. We had to dock a day's travel away to get Absko home. Diego, the cabin boy, Patty boy, and I made the trek with him. The rest of the crew was left with the boat and cargo. I always say cargo because I hated the thought of being a slaver. Never again did I try to profit from human enslavement.

Absko's family was elated to have him back. His father was a rich, powerful man, twice the size of anyone in the village, with bright green eyes. I'm guessing there was some sneaky European blood mixed in him. He had a wild, unkempt beard and spoke with a thunderous voice. I hope you get a mental picture of this man. He was jovial and generous, a dark-skinned Santa figure. At dinner that night, he gave us toast. He said, "These men have returned my son; I owe them my life!"

The village fed us and saw to our every need. He was happy to pay us not only for his son's safe return but also wanted every slave on our ship. We made a wise choice. Things do not always go as well as this transaction did. Accompanied by a troop of the tribe, we loaded the gold onto donkeys and made our way back to the ship. (Yea, it was a shit ton of gold.)

When we arrived back, we split the purse evenly. That raised my stature with the crew again. Selling our cargo after only a three-day voyage was excellent. Seeing our cargo be set free by Absko's tribe was spiritually uplifting. The next morning, I resigned from my position as captain and told the men to set sail without me. I was staying with my share of the gold and a couple of asses. I never saw or heard of *The Troyana* or (most) of her crew again. I spent the next thirty or so years slinging cock in Brazil.

ON and ON

Mother's Milk

My moral compass is continually changing. The person I am today doesn't need to steal to eat. When I was hungry, I felt no remorse about taking what I needed. I was tied to slave trading at one time. If not for a bit of luck, I would have sold those poor people and kept the money. I would have put that bit of guilt I felt about it in my back pocket until it slowly eased away. I have committed murder. I have fulfilled my sexual desires with unvirtuous women. Drank way too much. (Too many times to count.) I've cheated at cards and swindled a few casinos. I lay no claims to have led a virtuous life. I mostly try to do the right things. I am empathetic to others' needs. (Usually, after my needs are fulfilled.) I am also very good at forgiving myself after bad deeds are committed. I don't feel guilty for too long. Good? Bad? It's just survival. I'd rather be me with a bit of money in my pocket than Broke Me. I am also great at justifying why I may have done something less than a person with good character might have done. I have stated that for the record (in case you didn't already know). Cheating is something that came relatively naturally to me.

One of my lifelong enjoyments is going to horse races. I love the racetrack. Horse racing was a sport long before I was born. I can remember an annual event that was held in my small town. It was a favorite pastime of me and my brother to look at and touch every horse in the stable. Most times, the stable boys would shoo us away. We would run away laughing, only to return. "One day, we will get caught," Jareth wheezed, still catching his breath.

"Maybe your big slow ass!" I returned, bent over with my hands on my knees. "I am way too fast for these slow bastards! Besides, I only have to be faster than you."

"Then what? You leave me? Go home like I never existed?"

"Never, I'd never leave you!" I told him as I grabbed him close and noogied his head. "It's you and me forever."

We did get caught once, a few years later. When I turned to run away as we always did, an expensively dressed, dark-skinned bald man with gold teeth grabbed me when I ran almost directly into him.

"And what is diss?" he laughingly exclaimed. "Horse teefs?"

Jareth just stopped and looked at me. Our plan had always been just to run away and laugh. (Great plan.) The dark man's grip was like a vice, and he wasn't letting go. I, maybe for the first time in my life, didn't have shit to say. No smartass comeback, no curse words. I was a scared child. I, like Jareth, was frozen. He stared at us, his big dark eyes sizing us up. A full fifteen seconds went by, and then he laughed a colossal laugh and let us off the hook. "You boyz like the horses, eh? I might have a job for you." He loosened his grip off my shoulder and stepped back, giving us an opening to escape. We stood like statues, both excited to earn a few coins but more excited to be allowed in the stables. His name was Sly. It was a very fitting moniker.

The event lasted ten days, and we worked every day. We shoveled shit and fed them, but best of all, we washed and brushed all the horses. "I can't believe we get to do this." Jareth proclaimed while brushing a tall black mare named Clea.

ON and ON

"Lucky there isn't much to do on the farm; Dad would have never let us be here otherwise." I happily replied.

After a day or so and the horses became used to us, we could walk and even ride a short distance on a few of the older, gentile steeds. It didn't feel like work at all. Sly, our boss, on the ninth day, came to see us and pay us our wages. "Ye boys have worked hard for this money, and I give it to you without pause, but I know a way for you to turn it into much more."

"How could we do that?" Jareth skeptically asked before I could utter, "Yes!"

"Are you familiar with the term *past posting*? Also called late betting." Sly asked. Being simple farm boys, we had yet to learn what he was talking about.

"It's a form of betting when you already know the outcome," he said without further elaboration.

I asked, "Like knowing I am faster and can beat Jareth in a race?"

"Close, it's more like getting long-shot odds, say thirty to one, that Jareth will beat you."

"So, if I bet one coin, I'd get ten in return?" Jareth inquired.

"Better, more like if-n you wagered one coin to win thirty coins, but someone faster stepped into your place at the last moment and ran for you," Sly said with a smile.

Jareth was confused. "That's cheating," he said as he instinctually stepped back.

"Do as you wish, but in the last race today, Mothers Milk will win at thirty-five-to-one, longshot odds," Sly said as he dropped our payment on the table and turned to leave without looking at us. Before I could say to Jareth that I was going to bet my wages on Mother Milk, Sly walked back in and said, "Just in case ye boyz are daft, that lazy sow of a horse, Mother Milk. will be replaced at the last moment with a far younger unknown pony who is the fastest horse in my stable."

I was sold. I would have worked for free to be around the livestock for all those days. Jareth, being of more noble character, was less inclined to cheat someone. (Hard to believe we were brothers) He wouldn't even split the winning with me if I did win, and especially not split his with me if I lost. (Bastard!) I found an old drunk man at the racetrack to place my wager for me, but I had to agree to buy him a pint of beer in advance. I reluctantly agreed. (Dirty-ass old man robbing a child who was trying to rob a bookie.) I gave him my whole nine days' salary, minus the pint of beer, and he gave me my betting paper. The imposter, Mother Milk, won the race, and I had to find the old drunk to cash my ticket. The bastard wanted another pint to cash the ticket! Even worse, he tried to run off with my winnings after he saw how much I had won. Jareth was always bigger than me, and between the two of us, we tracked his drunk ass down and forcibly took what was mine. (Never trust a drunk!) The ruckus we caused by getting my money back did not go unnoticed, and a rumor quickly spread that Jareth and I were robbing old drunk men at the race.

"See what you have gotten us into? How are you going to spend that much money without Dad finding out? Jareth directed at me.

ON and ON

"Thought I'd just hide it and spend it gradually." was my un-fore thinking reply. "It'll be fine."

Jareth would not let it go after a week of shunning me, yelling at me, and trying to reason with me. I finally gave in, and we told my father what had happened. I had to talk to him before he went to town the next day. I knew someone would say something to him in the tavern about his sons beating up drunk old men.

"So, have you learned nothing?" Dad yelled at me. "Did you think god lets thieves in his kingdom?"

I stood my ground and said, "The odds makers cheat everyone; no one calls them thieves."

"Because someone else is doing it justifies it in your mind? Wrong is wrong!" He was getting angrier by the second. My sweet mother stepped in and asked how much I had won. They were both speechless when I revealed the total sum. Jareth saved the day and the beating I would get from my father by saying, "It's all for the farm, minus our wages."

My father dropped the rope he was holding (I believe he might have been planning to hang me with it.) "It was always meant for the family, "I lied. "We can buy whatever you think we need," I added.

My mother smiled and said, "It's a gift from the gods!" That was it. I put the coins in my father's hands, and they both hugged us. I learned a couple of valuable lessons that day. Only one person can keep a secret. Money will solve most problems, and the past posting was wrong. It was also profitable. It was a scheme I would use several times in my life. The essential rule to success was to be smart and never get greedy. Past posting can be used in a casino if you are fast enough. It could also get your hand cut off if you're too slow. (I don't know if my body parts grow back; I'm guessing no, but I have no intention of finding out for sure.) Past Posting could also be called *insider information.* We knew the horse pretending to be Mother Milk would win, so we past-posted and also had insider information. Win-win situation. It could be just insider information.

La Chaine Fide Forcats (The Chain Gang)

Being alive for over two thousand years wasn't always a good time. I've had my fair share of sadness, poverty, imprisonment, agony, and just shitty situations. I was once caught stealing a horse in the New Mexico territory and hung for two full days by only my neck with my hands strapped behind my back. I passed out and woke up, only to pass out again numerous times. I shit myself until there was nothing left in my intestines. Strangling to death isn't pretty. I was finally able to fray the rope by swinging back and forth until the rope snapped. I ran from that posse for six days before they caught and hung me. Eight days of bullshit for taking a horse. I knew the consequences of getting caught; there is no thrill like being chased. That's not by a long way the worst one. I spent over five years in a French prison for what was then called *"active blasphemy."* It sounds like I was leading the Satan for president parade. Nope, it's just religion.

At this time in history, the "house of carpets" controlled France. (Which has nothing to do with floor coverings, much like the Ming dynasty has nothing to do with vases). Everyone was devout Roman Catholic, and the church used religion to control the population. People have always been sinful and made to feel terrible for their humanity by the church. Not just in France but worldwide, and only in the last fifty years or so has that changed.

I was working at a small farm for a man named Jehon Belay. He was, on the surface, a good man. I liked him. He was a fair boss. Jehon was a soft-spoken man of few words. He needed help to carry on a conversation. He was afflicted with a touch of stuttering, also called stammering. The longer I knew him and the more comfortable he felt with me, the less he stammered. Jehon had a scrunchy face like everything was too close together. He was not ugly; his eyes, mouth, and nose were too close. He always looked like he was smelling something foul. He had broad shoulders and big feet but delicate, thin fingers. Nothing about him fit exactly right.

He was brilliant and was using science to buck the traditional methods of crop growth. With anything unexplainable in those days, you had to be very careful with success. Too much success would cause jealousy from other farmers, leading to scrutiny and possible threats of heresy. "Works of the devil" was the phrase that could be thrown at someone who was doing things differently from standard practices. Jehon and I had worked out a way to sell the excess produce that the landlord, taxes, and church didn't require. I would travel by night primarily for three days, ride to another small village, sell our goods wholesale to another merchant, and then bring back the money to be divided between us at a 70/30 split. I found the venture to be very fair. I also really liked the merchant's daughter. She was worth the three-day trip.

I rented a small room on Jehon's farm. We spent most days together. The work was long and hard but enjoyable. Jehon had a considerable library, and I could use it nightly. He always had some scientific experiment going. I can compare him to a poor man like Ben Franklin. He rarely slept, and his mind was always working on some problem.

ON and ON

Just like Ben, he loved women. Jehon was on the other end of the age spectrum. He didn't like older women. He did like to make and drink wine. Also, ales, grain alcohol, and anything he could ferment. He invented a newer way to plow. He developed a way to make his produce last longer. He had a vast greenhouse and grew exotic flowers. He had a homemade freezer he built out of hay and clay. (It was the first one I had ever seen.) I remember adding ice cubes to our lemonade in July. He was a quiet man, non-boastful, and didn't relate to other farmers in the region. He kept to himself, and I forced him to go to the local tavern with me.

On one of these trips to the watering hole, a problem arose, which was my fault. I drank too much (shocker). I got a little full myself and bragged about our product production. I had come a long way in my journey and did not usually behave in such an arrogant manner. I can admit I was wrong, but (constantly a but…): This fat, sloppy bug-eyed potato farmer was insulting Jehon in a very pissant sort of way. I wasn't having it. Consistently berating Jehon for lying about his inventions. Jehon hadn't said shit about anything he had invented, that wasn't his way. Gossip travels fast in small communities. Someone had said something about something they saw from the road on Jehon's property. Something they didn't understand or something of that nature. I remember Jehon offering Tubby some fertilizer to help his potato sizes. Jealousy was what it was. I then told this son of a bitch we could outgrow anything he had in half the space. I also offered "to shut his slobbery lips if he couldn't do it himself." After I knocked this fuckers teeth out, his brother (I was unaware of a brother.) Quietly stood behind me and stabbed me eight times in my kidney. I bled out in the back of Jehon's wagon on the way back to the farm. Jehon covered me with a blanket and would tend to my body the next morning. I woke up before him and started my day as usual. I had not at that time had someone witness my death and have to attend to my dead body. I didn't know how to react. I was covered with dry blood, and the wagon was too. There wasn't a hose to spray everything off. I was in an undeniable situation. Jehon and many of the customers in the tavern had seen me get stabbed. I'm sure Jehon inspected my wounds while I was passed out. He would have wanted to help with my injuries if he even could believe I had survived. If Jehon wasn't the man of science he was, I'm sure He would have taken me to be burned as a witch. (I one hundred percent did not want to be burned, fuck that!)

When Jehon saw me, he cried; he was genuinely excited to see me. He said, "I was sad you died."

He didn't ask me how or why. I said, "I heal fast."

He said something like "no shit." He told me, "There are things about you that never added up." He continued, "You look extremely young. You have had cuts on your hands from working, and those cuts are never there the next day." Then he looked directly at me, "The most unexplainable trait I have been wondering is why you are never hung over, ever?" He said, "It has always baffled me."

He would feel like total dogshit, and I was up and about cheery the next day. "It pissed me off," he said. He dug into a pile of papers and pulled out a chart of the number of drinks we had consumed and how he felt the next day when I felt normal. As I said, his mind was always working. I offered no explanation and just shrugged my shoulders.

ON and ON

Making Jehon be content to ponder on what he didn't know. My non-explanation did not satisfy him.

"You were dead, no pulse, no breathing, dead. Has this happened to you before?" He seriously inquired.

"You mean my drunk mouth causing me trouble? Of course, it has. You would think I'd learn a lesson." I said, trying to dodge the undodgeable situation.

"I'm not in the mood for your jokes." He stared at me. I was not wiggling off the hook. I wasn't sure how much I could tell him.

"I've never been stabbed like that before." I truthfully stated. "I heal incredibly fast; I've never had a hangover. I age very slowly. I'm not a demon. I don't know shit about any witchcraft or spells, I'm just me. The same man you have known all these years. I can leave if you feel uncomfortable with me staying. I want to stay and continue our partnership."

"I don't want you to leave. I want to understand how is it possible?"

"I honestly do not know; if I did, I would tell you." That statement was the most authentic thing I may have ever said to anyone. He was surprisingly content with my answer. I knew I was his only friend in the world. Choosing between the devil and loneliness wasn't that hard of a choice for him.

The problem of witnesses to my supposed killing was easily handled. I stayed at the farm and "healed" for about a month while Jehon spread the word of my miraculous survival. That left only one loose end. The murderous brother of the bug-eyed fat fuck. It consumed me. I had several plans and schemes to kill that fucker. To quote Marcellus Wallace from *Pulp Fiction*, I wanted to "get medieval on his ass." It was sort of medieval times, anyway, so I guess whatever I chose would count as such. I'm not the torture type, and he was just defending his brother. So maybe I could let it pass. (I know you don't believe a word of that nonsense.)

I was going to fuck him up. How to do it was the issue. I had to be smart and catch him unaware. I knew he would be armed and much bigger than me. I was positive I could beat his ass in a fistfight. But this wasn't a high school, "I'll meet you at the park" kind of fight. It was to stab you in the neck and watch you bleed out sort of fight. So, after weeks of planning, I walked into the same pub where the trouble all started, saw him sitting at a table, walked up to him, tapped him on the shoulder, and shoved my blade all the way to the handle right below his jawbone. I stared into his unsuspecting eyes as he realized what was happening to him and smiled at him. It may sound morbid, but I don't care in the least; he killed me, and I killed him right back!

After that, I lived life on the farm. I delivered our produce to the next village. I visited my lady friend and enjoyed the tranquil days on Jehon's farm. Jehon and I were still great friends, and I busted my ass doing the day-to-day farm work. We talked every day, we drank damn near every day, and Jehon did experiments (and probably still tracked my non-hangover days.) Life was great. He never openly asked about my talents, but I suspected he had a multitude of questions.

A problem came to light when Jehon was caught with a very young girl. A neighbor's daughter. Disgustingly young. (Very opposite of ol'

Ben.) The father wanted blood, and the church agreed. Jehon was going to be hung. No trial was needed; he was caught red-handed. The only way to save himself was to try to buy his way out. He offered the church a substantial sum of money, which they accepted, of course, and then they still tried to hang his perverted ass, anyway. I say *try* because good ol' Jehon slipped away. As I said, I liked Jehon Belay, and we had a good scheme going, but "what he was doing was wrong," as I repeated over and over when The Church questioned me about his whereabouts. Hanging him didn't bother me. In the end, most people get what they deserve. But then again...Jehon had taken me in and trusted me, taught me how to read charts/graphs and understand scientific reasoning, and we had shared many bottles of wine. He also showed me how to make wine. So, one night, I showed up at the jail around midnight and offered the jailer a sum he could not possibly refuse. I had brought Jehon a horse that was packed and ready for a very long journey, and farmer Jehon Belay disappeared into the night. Forever gone but never forgotten. I sometimes wonder where he ended up and if his unnatural, disgusting carnal desires did him in eventually. Even money bet: his dick got him killed, but I'm just guessing.

That's my backstory about going to jail; here is the rest. Someone in the clergy got to thinking, "Where did this farmer get all that money? Is there more we can grab?" Obviously, for the Lord's work (Of course.) It didn't take too long before an old, weathered, skinny bishop from the church, escorted by a few soldiers, came by the farm asking questions and snooping through Jehon's belongings. What pisses me off the most is the arrogance of the church officials. "Why this? Why that?" The bishop walked in and "acted with the authority of god." He then took all the wine. (BULLSHIT!) He didn't comprehend the drawings, calculations, nutrients, and pesticides Jehan was using, so they added heresy to the charges. (Obviously, the devil's work) and took the farm as well.

I worked with Jehon for close to fifteen years. We had a good relationship, and he confided his technology ideas to me. I understood what he was doing. When the church sent in the new farm owner, I was assigned to stay and help with the transition. Father Anton was our new superintendent. Old School wouldn't be what I called the new guy. Big-bellied but thin everywhere else. A fat, skinny guy. He was slovenly and dumb, but I would describe him as connected to someone important by family. He looked just like the monk on Belgium beer bottles, but skinny fat. He was a half-whit with super poor hygiene, but that was most everyone in those days, and he was just an unhappy man. He couldn't comprehend adding anything to the soil to help growth. "The Lord will provide "was his answer to my advice. To him, I was a nobody, which was true.

I held no lands or titles; I was just a hired hand. In hindsight, I should have handled skinny fats, feeble-minded ass wiser. I wouldn't have been carted off to prison if I hadn't argued and undermined him. I could have just left and started a new adventure elsewhere. Instead, I sabotaged him. I talked shit about him to whoever would listen at the tavern. A side note about the tavern: I was a legend for sticking that fool in the neck. He had been bullying pretty much everyone in the place for years. Everyone was afraid of him and hated him. (Well, good for me.)

ON and ON

My anger towards the church manifested itself towards Mr. Fat Skinny. I threatened to beat his monk haircut having ass. I made him look stupid several times. It was too easy, and I couldn't help myself (I was still working on my personal growth.) I was a smart ass to him all the time. The monk was a little sneakier than I gave him credit for; he had been writing a journal of our interactions. I didn't think the fucker could read. That bit me in the ass. Why was I shocked when soldiers showed up and took me away? Riding in the back of that cart, manhandled a bit, I knew I had fucked up. I thought maybe I'd take a few lashes or something of that nature. They took me straight to prison. "Active blasphemy" was my charge, which was a loose term the church used to charge anyone with anything they wanted (basically bullshit.) Old Fat Skinny man must have been related to someone! He tattled on me. He had written verification of my "ungodly" behavior. He had eyewitness accounts and signed confessions from the place I considered myself a "legend" I should have never entered that fucking tavern! Those are great words for everyone to live by: don't go to the bar, nothing good ever happens after midnight, and one more won't hurt. (Sound familiar?)

There was no reason to hold a trial since I owned no land or titles. It didn't matter what I had to say to defend myself. I was a peasant in their eyes. I honestly was a peasant, even if I didn't feel like one. There was no bill of rights, I was fucked, simple as that! A judge didn't pound his gavel and declare my punishment. There was no court nor jury. The original bishop, Father Todd, showed up. He sneered at me with a shame on you look on his face and basically said, "Take this shit-talking punk ass away,"

It wasn't a prison-like today, or the one Edmond Dante was put in called the Chateau D'if in *The Count of Monte Cristo*. It was a small castle dungeon. Dirt floor, very damp, and musty. I'm sure animals had been kept there not long before I arrived. It wasn't very prison-like, and I broke out of that bitch in less than two hours, but I had two fundamental problems. Both had their own set of issues. First of all, I was naked. Can you believe that? They took my clothes and threw me in that dungeon, butt-ass naked. Okay, so I could steal some clothes, possibly. The other problem was the castle had a moat. Seriously. A fucking moat, like in the fairy tales. A big, deep-ass moat. Filled with crocodiles! (Not really, but since it sounds like a fairy tale, let's add crocodiles.)

I could pull out two rotting bars from the castle dungeon's gate, carefully sneak naked to the moat, avoiding any giant man-eating reptiles, and swim across the ice-cold water to freedom. Where I was immediately shot with an arrow just below my right shoulder blade and dragged back. That shit hurt. So did the ass beating my guards gave me and the lashing I took a week later.

So, having my attitude firmly adjusted, "I chilled/that's right I chilled" (a line from one of my favorite 1990's songs, *Walking in the Rain*. In the song, the singer busts his girl cheating, I was just busted up in general.) As I've stated earlier, I heal quickly. Healing of the body is very different from the healing of my mind. I did not want to be shot or whipped again, ever! I was both shot and whipped again but not for a long ass time. The castle was just a stop along the way to my eventual destination. The guards put me on what is now known as a chain gang. Then called la chaine fide forcats. (a little multi-lingo humble brag.) It

ON and ON

was a prison labor farm. It was rough. I was left inside the gate with one piece of paper. It listed my name, crime, and sentence of five years. Until I read the paper, I had no idea about the length of my sentence. Looking back, I was still very arrogant. My thoughts included, "All these fucks will be dead in five years, to this chain gang can't hold me."

Being naked makes it very hard to stand tall. It was also cold, so there's that too. I was angry. Angry at the church, angry at the fat skinny snitch, angry at Jehon's dick for causing all of this. But I was furious at myself for being such a dumb-ass fool.

Still naked, I walked into camp. No one spoke to me. No one gave me directions. Nobody even looked at me. I found a place to lie down and was awakened by the shuffling of men in the early morning. When everyone mainly had left, I found a pair of rotten pants in the dirt and followed. I jumped in the chow line and was given a very meager meal of cold oats. And then off to work. To be honest, the labor wasn't that bad. We were building a road. Come to find out, it is a really, really long road. I fell into the norms of prison life. I was fighting for everything I needed to survive. Take what I need from the weaker and avoid the stronger. The guards could give two shits about men who died. Less to feed.

Like prison today, we socially segregate ourselves by race and class. I grouped with the rest since I wasn't French, Muslim, or German. Men from the Mediterranean, Norwegian, and Celtic regions. My segregated group included three giant Norwegian fellows. Each of them was 6 foot 4-sh. Nobody wanted to fuck with them. After a couple of months of working, observing (and staying close to the

Vikings), I acquired the necessities I needed to survive. I made friends with this interesting man named Alfredo. He was a mixed breed. He never would say where he was from, but I assume he was Basque. I've met several men of his general demeanor in my travels and liked them all. All smiles every day. Hot as hell? All smiles. Raining? Smiles. Cold? Smiles. It's contagious.

Alfredo was a thin, short man with thick, flowing dark hair. He had a presence that could be felt when he was near. He had a contagious laugh and bright, dark, intelligent eyes; even when angry about something, he seemed generally happy. I found myself not so pissed about digging hard ass ground. Also not so pissed about my current situation. It was just a new experience, a fucked experience but not as bad as it could have been. Alfredo was also a sneaky little bastard. He could steal your shoes off your feet. Talk himself out of a fight or stab you in the neck if your neck needed stabbing. (The neck is an excellent stabbing place.) We became close friends. Spending every day together made life easier. We talked constantly about escaping. I came close to telling him my secret but never did. We constantly battled with the arrogant fucking French. (I still don't like them) stole food and ale from the Germans. How they could make ale on a chain gang still eludes me. (I still love German-brewed beer.)

I always hid behind and took good care of our giants. Those Norwegian boys came in clutch on numerous occasions. We always made sure they were well-fed. It's incredible how you can sneak off to forage or hunt. Well, it's not that amazing because our guards didn't take a roll call during the day, only at night. A couple of criminals did try to escape but were always apprehended and got the shit beat out of

ON and ON

them. A few were simply shot. We mostly ate well. Some sort of meat was always available to catch or sometimes steal from nearby farms. Many of the fights between us and the rest of the crew were over food or what they accused us (Alfredo) of stealing. Our big men always held tight for us, and besides a few small fistfights. (Once Alfredo stabbed this Frenchie in his eye with a sharp stick), we mainly were well protected. That French frog tried to ambush Fredo, but since he couldn't see out of one eye, Fredo beat the shit out of him and took his shoes. It sounds funny now, but stealing his shoes seemed perfectly normal then. (Times change.)

We called our Norwegian buddies "Le Geants," French for giants. They were always together. They looked very similar and could have all been brothers or at least related. Astrid, Oskar, and Magnus were their names, or something very close. Huge men with dark blond hair and large beards. It took almost a year before I could understand a word they said. Astrid was the oldest and ran the show. They rarely bickered and mostly followed the directions of the guards. I say mainly because a few times they refused to work. Not often, but ten or twelve times, I remember Astid walking early in the morning before we were to get started to the guard's camp, returning and saying, "No work today." No one said shit; I just went back to sleep. It must have been some cultural holiday of sorts. The guards were either ready for a day off or didn't wanna fuck with Le Geants. I was cool either way.

I've seen movies like *Cool Hand Luke* where the guards were mounted on horses with rifles ready to shoot anyone starting trouble or not working fast enough. It wasn't like that for us. Our guards did have horses and rifles, but only one was a dick. The others have faded from my memories, but not "Le Vigilo." He wasn't the captain of the guards but tried to be. His name translates to being vigilant, but it was a mockery of him. It means taking shit too far, doing too much, and being a try-hard. (A term I've heard teen-agers use.) A better name might have been "the little dick." He had little man disease and was covering up his genital shortcomings by how he behaved and looked. If aviator sunglasses had been invented, he would have worn them. He reminds me of "Chet," the obnoxious older brother in the movie *Weird Science*. We didn't have the technology for a flat-top haircut, but he would have had one. He would have driven a huge lifted 4x4 pick-up truck and wore a sleeve of tribal tattoos as well.

He was constantly pushing for more work. We had a simple system to build our road. We would dig a level path a little less than half a kilometer. A cart was pulled in loaded with small gravelly rocks. We spread the rocks into the dugout earth, and that section was done. It took about a month to do each section. Many obstacles blocked our path, trees, large hills, swampy lands, giant ass boulders, and so on. Sometimes, half of the men would be digging and half filling. Other times, men were taken ahead to clear obstacles in the path. Le Vigilo ensured we stayed on task, which we mostly did. A man or two would sneak off to forage for food or try to find whatever is needed to brew German beer. There were very few incidents in which whoever left did not return in time for bed check.

Le Vigilo would go on a hunt looking for anyone who left the group; no other guard gave a fuck. They would get a small portion of whatever was brought back, and all would be good. Magnus was once caught bringing a deer into camp. Le Vigilo made a huge stink about it and

ON and ON

wanted the entire deer and Magnus to take ten lashes. Astrid would not allow it. "Take the deer, you little piece of shit, but you will not touch him!"

Le Vigilo was livid and yelled, "He was caught red-handed; he must pay the price!"

There was a moment of calm silence, and it looked like all hell might break loose. The two men were stuck in a dead-eye staring contest, neither giving an inch. Finally, Le Vigilo folded, took the deer and walked away. Later that evening Alfredo showed up with cooked venison. (Sneaky fuck.) After the altercation, Le Vigilo was always lurking around the Vikings, looking for any reason to punish them. They were caught for minor infractions and had rations taken away or put on more burdensome duties.

Tensions were building up, and then one day, Le Vigilo was gone. Had he been reassigned? He had never missed a day of riding his stupid horse too close or fucking with us. The other guards came by and asked us a series of questions individually. They didn't appear to be overly concerned. He vanished. (Fuck yes!!) I asked Oskar, "What happened to Le Vigilo?" I specifically asked Oskar because he was the mildest mannered of the three Vikings, and if there was a hierarchy between them, he was the lowest.

I remember him casually saying, "I'm sure he will show up... eventually."

It was the way he emphasized "eventually" that made me know for sure he wasn't coming back. We got back to building our road. The weather turned warmer, and the wheel of life continued to roll. The mystery was solved about six weeks later while the entire team was moving a huge boulder from our intended path. When the team finally pushed the stone aside, we found Le Vigilo crushed underneath it. The rock was so massive that no part of him was visible on any side. It took fifteen men with ropes to move that huge ass chunk of stone. I'm sure "Le Geants" killed Le Vigilo. There is an old saying, "Fuck around, fuck around, you won't be around." Le Vigilo fucked around. I have no idea how they moved that boulder, just the three of them. Why did they do it in our path so he was sure to be found? Maybe it was a warning to the other guards? Every whisper in camp blamed the Vikings. The Germans sent over beer to them. Everyone took a turn quietly, acknowledging them for dropping a house on the witch. Not one of them ever took credit for doing it. They didn't even smile when the beer arrived. So glad they were on my side.

The thought of escape was what kept us going. Just the idea of escaping and planning how we would do it. Where we would go, we decided to make a break for it one night when the moon was just a sliver and the weather was getting warmer. We had been timing the guards' patrols for about a month. We made our attempt right after the first guard shift. We timed it perfectly, but Alfredo twisted his knee about a mile from camp due to the lack of moonlight. He tried to tough it out, but eventually, I had to carry him, and we had to sneak back in. It was much more difficult getting back in than getting out. We laughed about getting caught breaking into prison many times, mostly when we were drunk on German beer.

After about three years, my scientific knowledge paid off while I tried to turn a swampy area into our road to hell. Using drainage techniques,

ON and ON

I learned on Jehon's farm, we transformed the swamp into a workable muddy area and made it through. After that, I was done with hard labor. I was a surveyor. I could not possibly do the work I needed to do without Alfredo. So, he was allowed to be on my team of surveyors. Eventually, I was able to include my Viking friends, too. Turns out they are excellent horsemen. Our work turned out to be essential, and we were given our tents and first food rights. Of course, it pissed off the French. (Ha-ha!) We even made a couple of the guards our friends. Most days, we rode horses on a ten-mile circle, looking for the easiest path for our road. We started referring to it as our road once we were surveyors. (Top dogs!)

I went from angry to very happy and fulfilled in prison. (Rehabilitated? Maybe not quite.) One day, Alfredo tells me a farmhouse is nearby, and we should go check it out and grab a few chickens. I'm one hundred percent down to check it out, so we sneak away. Upon arriving at the cottage, we first see sisters working in a garden. I tell Alfredo, "Chickens only, don't approach the women." He nods okay but heads straight for them. Again, someone's dick is going to cause me trouble.

Alfredo was a charmer; I'll give him that. In a matter of minutes, both ladies are smiling and laughing. I take that as my cue to join. Chickens be damned. Small talk ensues, and just as things heat up, a wagon appears on the horizon. (Shit, time to go.) Alfredo convinces them to meet us later that evening, and we bounce. Back at our tent, Alfredo pulls out a dozen eggs and a bottle of wine. Where he got them? I have no idea. I was with him the whole time. I never saw eggs or wine. It's still a mystery. Even more of a mystery is the sliced ham folded into a nice napkin he pulled from his pocket. Sadly, the sisters never showed up that evening. The thought of meeting two convicts after dark must have sounded better in the daylight. We joked that we got the better end of the deal. If we had to choose, a good bottle of wine and a meal was better anyway. (Lies we tell ourselves.)

The road plans instructed us to follow a specific path that led us - get this - a huge fifty-mile circle. It's a famous road now, no shit. It's called A86. Look it up! It circles Paris. I was on the prison labor team that built that bastard. They made us do it to keep us busy.

About two months after we completed the road, Alfredo was killed by a tree that fell on us during a severe thunderstorm. We were in a shelter and had no idea until it was too late. I broke my back and pelvis. The Norwegians lifted the trees off us, but it was too late. I was left to die by the guards. They had no time for offering my peasant ass any medical aid. They did leave me a half bottle of wine to ease my suffering. (I always thought that was nice.) So, the next day, I walked away a free man, not even a scar. Alfredo wasn't so lucky. I've since returned to Paris and driven on the much-improved road we built. I have a sense of pride and sadness for our accomplishments. France has so many attractions to see, from museums to iconic structures. The food is terrific, and the women are sexually liberated. The wine flows, but my favorite thing is that damn road and, of course, my memories of Alfredo and my giants. I helped build something that has stood the test of time and encountered remarkable men I will always cherish.

ON and ON

<u>Gangsters</u>

Throughout my lifetime and history, the class system was firmly in place. In almost every country in the world, this is true. Who you were was who you would always be. Born poor, die poor. Exceptional talent was needed to lift a person into a higher class. Not being in the lowest classes would mean more ability to succeed and survive. It took me almost a hundred years to understand that if I wanted not to be poor, I had not to be poor already or very talented at something. I was not an artist or musician. I didn't have anything to offer as exceptional. I was likable, and while being liked is excellent, which might get me laid, it did not raise my economic status. Hard work is good, but more is needed. I had to have something that stood out, and it had to be repeatable about every twenty-five years. After about a quarter of a century, I look too young to continue living in my current position. On some occasions, I could carry some wealth with me in the form of gold or even livestock. Other times, I only had the clothes on my back. The answer to my problem was much more straightforward than it appeared. I didn't need to be high-born. I only needed to act like I was high-born. Simple. Stupid! Once I began acting like I wasn't a peasant, I was no longer a peasant. I've been caught in my scam; It hasn't always gone as planned. I've left towns just ahead of the governor's army or the church and also just ahead of a pissed-off husband.

I chose carpentry, farming, plumbing, and even blacksmithing as my professions and became a perceived expert in that field. Then I would buy a property, and that was that! I didn't always use this system. I sometimes joined the army, but never as a simple soldier, always as a professional soldier from another country. In Central America and Africa, I was often given the position of Captain or above. I was even the president of a gold mining company in South Africa. I've tried law enforcement a few times, but it's never a good fit. I'm better at breaking laws. I ran moonshine during prohibition while serving as Hamilton County's deputy sheriff in New York state.

That's not the only time I made money illegally, but what is legal is often defined by the times, who's in charge, and especially the location. Many things that were illegal in the past are lawful now and vice versa. Slavery was a common practice for thousands of years. Prostitution is both legal and illegal, depending on where you are. Drug use has been a common occurrence throughout history. So, providing some rum-to-rum drinkers sounded fun, and it was.

The 1920s, just after WW1, was a great time to be in America. I had avoided WW1 as much as possible. I sold a boatload of stolen ammo to some rebel forces in Italy. (Another story for another time.) After a couple of years, I parlayed that money into a couple of fruitful investments and lined my pockets with cash. I also purchased some coastal property I planned to sit on until the right buyer came along. I was ready for my next adventure and bought a berth on an ocean liner headed to New York City.

The cross-Atlantic trip was long and mostly relaxing. Most days, I sat on the first-class top deck enjoying the sun and ocean breezes. The evenings would consist of dining in the stuffy but well-furnished restaurants offered to high-paying voyagers. It was a three-month trip, and I spent most days doing nothing much more than laying around, eating, drinking, and chasing arrogant women. (Not difficult.) My boredom got the best of me, and I also explored the ship. The vessel's technology amazed me; it differed significantly from the ships I had previously sailed aboard. One of my exploratory walks took me to the lowest levels of the ship. Moving shadows caught my attention as I walked down dark, steamy corridors. I wasn't alone. It only enhanced my peripherals because any number of crewmen could be working in this part of the ship. I wouldn't be in trouble if caught, but I knew this area was restricted from passengers.

Shushed voices tingled my spidey senses, and I stopped to listen. A man appeared in front of me. It was too dark to see him clearly, but he was large and foul-smelling. "This part of the ship is off limits to….."

That's all I remember. Someone had hit me in the back of my head with something heavy. I awoke to a minor headache and dry blood on my shirt. I was crumpled in a small hallway and pushed against the wall. I had been robbed and stripped down to nothing but my underclothes. Fuckers even took my shoes. (Maybe shoe theft is common in all eras.) I stood up and started walking back to my room when I noticed my ring was gone.

My heart sank in a combination of butterflies and panic. I immediately felt the back of my head. There was no open wound; it was only a touch tender. Was it a glancing blow or, more sinister, something hard enough to kill? I had long since decided the ring wasn't the secret to my superpower, but I still wanted it back. I continued back to my room. I didn't get mugged for much money, but my pride was wounded, and I wanted to reclaim my custom leather shoes, but I mainly wanted my punk ass ring! While getting redressed, I tried to decide where to begin. All I knew was that one of my assailants was very large and smelled of bad dental hygiene. I never saw his face; would I recognize his voice? They had taken my money of course but also my clothes and shoes.

I'm a very average-sized person, so anyone my size was a suspect. I concluded it wasn't one of the first-class passengers; why would they steal my shit? So, I needed to walk through the ship's "coach" clientele. Did I happen upon stowaways? Was some terrorist attack being planned? (Most likely not.) I had the element of surprise on my side. The blow to my head was a kill shot, and I'm sure I was assumed dead. I decided to go back to the scene of the crime. They would need to come back and dispose of my body. They would come back to toss me overboard. I didn't like my odds; I needed a way to take them individually. I decided to hide in the shadows and wait for them to come to dispose of my body. I hoped the big one was just the muscle and not the brains. Maybe I could reason with them, "Give me back my ring, and you keep everything else; I won't say shit." (I could also ask nicely for my shoes.) I didn't believe it would go so easy. Around midnight, I heard two voices coming towards me.

"He will be just ahead, " one voice said in Italian.

Another voice just grunted.

"Did you push the body against the sidewall like I told you?"

"I did everything you told me." A low grumbling reply came, also in Italian.

ON and ON

"*Dove cazzo e, stupido?*" *Where the fuck is he, stupid.* The voice was harsh and demanding, also much louder than necessary.

I heard a shuffling of clothes, maybe the big guy gesturing with his shoulders, something like, I don't know. Next, I heard a smack, an open hand slap to the skin. Then I heard a much heavier punch and saw a man slide on the ground past my hiding space, a man wearing my clothes and my shoes.

"Find him yourself, *pezzo di merda!*" *Piece of shit.* The big man growled like he had a mouth full of gravel, and I heard him stalking away heavy-footed. As the Italian thief sat rubbing his jaw, I emerged from the shadows and delivered a solid knock-out punch to the other side of his jaw. I caught him on the button and put him to sleep long enough to take back my shoes and ring. I thought about taking my clothes back and leaving him as naked as he had left me, but while rummaging through his pockets, I found my wallet with an extra thousand dollars in it. (Winner, winner.) I left him on the floor and walked in the other direction, just in case the monster changed his mind and decided to come back. I hastily returned to first class, found the bar, ordered a round for the house, and danced the soles off my custom leather shoes.

I will never forget the feeling of sailing by Ellis Island and seeing the Statue of Liberty for the first time. Humbling. America had always been the land of opportunity, but in 1920, it was booming. After wandering for a month or so, hitting all the speakeasies, making a few connections, and generally following my dick around, I found myself at a resort in the Adirondack Mountains, which is upstate New York.

This place was spectacular. Tiptop everything from the food to the women. Everything was over the top. Millionaires, politicians, gangsters, and movie stars are all there just to party. This place was Vegas before Vegas existed: jazz and big band music bumping from multiple bars. Roulette wheels spinning, dice games, and all sorts of card games.

After a few days, I was ready to make solid business connections. Prohibition had just made alcohol illegal (the stupidest law ever passed), and running booze was very lucrative. Everybody saw easy money and wanted a piece of the pie. My cash reserve was holding firm, especially after winning big on a few bets placed on black number twenty hitting on the roulette wheel. The wheel was rigged. I just needed to grease the hands of the croupier and not get greedy. (I have all the time in the world; why get greedy?) With money and wine flowing, I had to find out who was who. I trusted no one. Most of the guests were just on vacation. The movie stars egotistically ass's wanted to be seen and photographed. Millionaires don't give a fuck; most were trust fund blue blood. That just left the politicians and gangsters.

The gangsters were a far safer play. They are much more honest and more straightforward to read. They want money. Politicians are sneaky, slimy, lying fucks. (Easy choice.) I told you earlier that I read people very well; I also don't fuck with people who will screw you over just because they think they are better than you. Until just recently, it was Monarchs, royal families, and clergy who believed the world revolved around them. I add politicians into that group of bitches. So, I befriended a couple of hard gangsta-ass Mofos, and here is where the story begins.

ON and ON

You can always find a dive bar just off the beaten path. The hard-working staff need a place to live and unwind. I was able to buy a few rounds, make a few friends, add a couple of extra dollars tipping, and get the information I needed after about a week of bullshitting around with some of the help. Bartenders and cocktail servers know all the scuttle.

I made sure to insert myself into a group of gentlemen that contained a tall, handsome guy named Johnny Rosselli. He liked horses, so I bought a horse. He enjoyed swimming at odd hours, late and early, and so did I. And so on. Eventually, he approached me about our seemingly random similar interests. Johnny was very likable. He was funny and very easygoing. Very smart and extremely handsome. Women flocked to him, especially the movie stars; a man could get fat on all his leftovers. He later became known as the Gentleman Gangster. He moved to California and ran the West Coast interests for the Chicago families for years. We became fast friends. He knew the pulse of the Adirondack resorts. He knew every fun thing going on and inserted himself into everything worth doing very easily. We had a blast together gambling, drinking, fishing, and chasing skirts. (I chased, and he collected.) Finally, he confided to me that he was leaving, "I have to refill my bank account, enough fucking off, and I need to get back to work." (This was what I was waiting for, let's run some rum!)

I had earned Rosselli's trust after giving him a heads-up about a man lurking about trying to break into the group. (Not nearly as sly as me.) My croupier buddy tipped me off that this bastard was a federal agent from Michigan named Fillion. He was playing both sides; he was a rat-faced greasy slimeball. Giving Rosselli that info solidified our friendship. Rosselli played it very cool. Fillion was never outed and was allowed to hang on the fringes of our group. Only some of the way in, but not pushed out. I heard a rumor that Rosselli even used the friendship to avoid a raid soon after we all left.

Later that year, I can't be one hundred percent sure who ordered the hit. A meeting was set up between the two men. After meeting in New York, someone shot that fucker in his oily rodent face; my money is on the Gentleman gangster.

Mr. Rosselli needed a runner to drive from New York Harbor, sail to Nassau Harbor, and meet with a bootlegger named Willy McCoy. The plan's brilliance was that the driver was also to be hired as a deputy in the nearby Hamilton County sheriff's department. Hamilton County is where our resort is located. I fit the bill perfectly; I looked the part, spoke several languages, and could sail. And the most significant need of all, I wasn't a greedy fuck. The total trip took two days. (It reminds me of my trips to Jehon.) It was about a six-hour drive down to the harbor in New York and a three-hour boat trip. I would drive down, get a little rest, and then, around midnight, sail the schooner out to Nassau. Sometimes, I'd spend the next day there and then wait until dark and make the return trip. Easy peasy.

Now, Willy McCoy was a legit businessman who sold his charter boat business just after the temperance movement took off. He was a forethinker. Most loads with other distributors were packed in hefty wooden boxes. Willy wrapped his product in paper and burlap. Almost half of the weight, which meant I could carry more liquor. Another bonus was that McCoy's alcohol was always what it claimed to be.

ON and ON

Never watered down, never poisoned, consistently top-shelf stuff. The term "The Real McCoy" started because of Willy's booze. As prohibition continued, other distillers would add harmful ingredients to enhance color or increase volume. People would go blind or even die from ingesting the poison added to the alcohol. Willy had many connections and used them always to have what was needed available.

McCoy always wore a big Panama hat and a very loud silk shirt. I never saw him in long pants. He always wore sandals like the original Tommy Bahama. Everything was easy with him. It was a well-run, slick operation. Sometimes, Rosselli would accompany me on the trip, and we would stay a week or so. There were always many beautiful women in Nassau. He never rode back to Hamilton County with me. That was too much heat if I were to get pulled over. I never even got a second look from law enforcement. Why would a sheriff's cruiser draw any attention? I made tens of thousands of dollars and hundreds of thousands for the Gentleman. Like all things in life, everything great must end. William McCoy's distribution enterprise caught the attention of the Coast Guard, and when they fired a six-pound shell at him, he closed shop. He was arrested six months later but never gave any names and retired peacefully somewhere in the Caribbean. (He may have started the Tommy Bahama clothing line?)

At about this time, the federal government started cracking down on illegal alcohol. With task forces going after runners and producers, it became tougher not to get caught. The increased attention from the federal government caused bootlegging to get dangerous, and getting killed for pennies became a widespread occurrence. Real murderers replaced the more peaceful, business-minded gangsters. The new bosses were hard-core, stone-cold killers. On one of my last Nassau runs, a group of these men intercepted me. They applied a little physical force, but I had no fear and gave no information except to tell them who I worked for and that I had a fantastic memory. The Rosselli name-drop changed their attitudes, and I was allowed to continue on my way. I never mentioned that encounter to anyone until now. (Honestly, I forgot about it)

Not long after busting bootleggers and gangsters, the federal government came after the corrupt politicians. That's when shit got crazy. Just a heads up, I quit running rum just after Willy McCoy got pinched. It became a job, and I wanted an adventure. Plus, I didn't need the money, and Rosselli was moving out to the west coast. I resigned from police work as well and reinvented myself. I have to clean up and finish the story, so I will give you a very brief, simplified explanation of what happens next.

So a big baller named Arnie Rothstein (yeah, that guy, the one who rigged the World Series) tried to muscle in and take over all upper New York distribution. The five families didn't like that shit, and Arnie got popped. Rumor has it that Rosselli ordered the hit, but I don't think he had that kind of juice. I'm not saying he couldn't have done it, but I doubt it. Rothstein held on for a few days but eventually died from a gunshot wound to his stomach. Arnie was a super overweight, snaggle-toothed man. Over the top, loud and untouchable. So, he thought. He was connected to the New York political machine. He was backed by the Mayor of New York, a man named Jimmy Walker (not the dyno-mite actor from *Good Times*). Jimmy was a weasel of a man and a stone-cold killer. Together, these two men ran the city, legally and illegally. So, taking over upstate New York should have been an easy transition. But like always, things change, and greed is very powerful. When Rothstein was killed, Jimmy Walker had to take a step back and re-evaluate his options. While Walker was dealing with his business, other more pressing shit was about to drown him. Franklin Delano Roosevelt, FDR!!, was governor at the time, and he knew Jimmy Walker was corrupt (as did EVERYONE), so he prosecuted the whole city. FDR was a *bad* no-nonsense man who did not give a fuck about anyone who was not doing the right thing. He was very ambitious and saw correctly that cleaning up New York was the big ticket to bigger and better things. Later in 1933, when he became president, he repealed prohibition and put an end to all that bullshit. Just a side note: good politicians, kings, and bishops are few and far between. FRD was incredible. I know he put America's best interests first. Still, he did open a slippery slope for presidential executive orders that have become broader and more ridiculous as time passes. (Just one small political opinion of mine)

I was only in New York for about four years at that time, and luckily, I didn't get shot, stabbed, or have my life threatened (except for that one time I mentioned.) The stock market crash in 1933 took most of my profits from bootlegging but not all of it, and I was able to recover financially and move on.

<u>Diego</u>

I have sailed many times for many reasons. In the early to mid-fifteenth hundreds, nations were exploring newfound lands across the entire globe. Mainly for money or strategic strongholds to outmaneuver enemy countries. Under the weak ass guise of saving lost souls or bringing new religion to foreign people. Only the truest in faith believed the bullshit being served. Kings wanted gold and natural resources. Explorers wanted fame and wealth. Mostly fame. Many rich, entitled, arrogant bastards set sail as explorers only to end up dead and forgotten. I joined one of these explorations in 1527, sailing out of Spain. Spanish King Charles V sent Panfilo de Narvaez to explore, conquer, and settle La Florida. (The Gulf Coast of Florida.) He also sent a bookworm by the name of Cabeza de Vacca.

Panfilo was a hard-core believer in his mission of religious exploration. He was very devout. Cabeza was more realistic and money-driven. They were at odds most of the time. I, along with six hundred soldiers, five ships, and a handful of colonists, set sail for the new world.

The first leg of our voyage took about six weeks and was truly uneventful. We landed in what was then called Hispaniola, now modern-day Haiti and the Dominican Republic. It was a tropical paradise. Our captains wanted to buy horses and men. They also set upon building a sixth ship.

Tropical beaches and rum made for easy days. Many of the Spanish people meant for La Florida decided to stay. Some soldiers also

ON and ON

decided to stay and left the ranks, never to be seen again. (I could care less) I was hired not as a soldier but as someone who could communicate with the indigenous population we were to encounter. I found the women of Hispaniola liked to communicate.

Finally, after six weeks or so, the ship was finished, and having lost so many of our passengers, our captains decided it was time to scoot. We didn't find the horses we needed, so instead, we set sail for what is now Cuba. I was to find at least one hundred horses once we arrived.

The sea turned angry a little over halfway through our voyage. Not a little angry, but pissed the fuck off. We encountered a massive hurricane. Of course, hurricanes didn't have names back then, but this one was Large Marge or Ivan the Terrible. It tore two of our ships apart in less than an hour. I mean ripped planks off and threw them away. The furious winds blew so hard that one of the boats was lifted out of the water and disintegrated. After the storm, the event became labeled "God's will." I call it hurricane alley in hurricane season, but we didn't know that shit then.

The other ships regrouped and sailed to Cuba; somehow, I had not been blown overboard, but many souls had not been that lucky. Bodies could be seen floating as far as I could see. Then, horribly, the sharks came! The attacks began as a ripple in the water, and a body was sucked under. Tiny red bubbles rise to the top of the water. Then the feeding frenzy began. Thousands of fins moving across the top of the now-calm waters. In a matter of minutes, the sea boiled in foam and blood. Then shrieks! Horrible-horrible noises, not everyone was dead.

We threw out a few ropes, and I remember pulling in two soldiers. Otherwise, there was nothing to be done but watch and cry.

Physically malnourished, desperately low on water, and emotionally scarred, we floated into the Havana harbor. Ships needed to be repaired. More men needed to be hired. And I had to purchase one hundred horses somehow. I wanted to find a bottle of Cuban rum, a nice cigar, a couple of senoritas, and a nice shady spot and drink away the memory of my last thirty days. But, as always, I was alive! So, fuck it. Horses, not whores it was.

I eventually found a ranch near the harbor and met with a short, very old, wrinkled-faced man willing to part with the horses I needed. He looked at me very strangely and whispered, "*Si senor Espectro Pote*," which translates to Yes, Mr. Ghost can. I stood in silence while I tried to process why he would call me a ghost can. I am light-complected but more red than white. Then it hit me, the old man was fucking Diego!! The cabin boy from the Troyana! Holy shit! It's like a comedian who brings back a joke from the beginning of his show and inserts it as his last catch punchline. I don't know how many years it had been, but more than sixty. I pretended not to understand what he was talking about; Diego wasn't buying my bullshit. I never acknowledged to him that it was me. I did listen to his story. Diego said, "After taking my split of the gold from Rio De Janeiro. We sailed the ship to Cuba. There was a fight between the crew about where to go next. I didn't trust anyone. You and Palos were gone. I had no protection; I slipped away the first night we arrived. After a week of hiding, I saw the Troyana sail away. I had no choice but to stay. I bought this ranch and have raised cattle and horses ever since."

ON and ON

He insisted on me staying for dinner and rum while telling me about his family. I fabricated a lie. I told him and his family, "My grandfather would tell this story about sailing to Brazil. He told us about a fight where a dear friend was killed. He hated the captain, and there was a mutiny. He also said he returned an enslaved person to his family. It felt more like an embellished fable than truth. I guess we should have believed him."

Diego listened respectfully but, in the end, simply replied, "Si, si senor Espectro Pote." which translates to *fucking liar*. I played it as cool as possible; I rarely saw a person from my past. Damn, he was old as hell. Suddenly, a hurricane and shark attacks didn't feel so traumatic. Diego's withered, over-baked apple face seemed worse.

Diego would not take my money for the horses; he insisted that if I hadn't shared my gold, he would have never become who he became. He looked at me, then at my hands, and quietly said, "Tu anillo, solo he visto uno." *Your ring, I've only seen one like it.* (Shit, he had a point.) I called him "a loco old man" and tossed the bag of coins at his granddaughter's feet and rode the fuck off. Riding away, I was glad we pulled him back into the boat after he was thrown overboard. I may have a little *Kung-Fu* David Carradine in me after all.

After completing my horse-wrangling task, I needed time to gather myself and decided not to travel to Florida. I wanted to avoid getting on a boat again for a while. Still, Cuba is an island, so I inevitably sailed again after six weeks or so. The story of Panfilo and Cabeza's travels gets pretty good, and I wish, in hindsight, that I had continued traveling with them.

From Cuba to La Florida, another hurricane took all but two ships. They landed near Tampa Bay and were attacked by local Indians. (As you know, I want no part of that) Panfillo was killed, and Cabeza and the twenty or thirty soldiers that were left went on an almost decade-long hike across half of America. Cabeza somehow becomes a healer or some shit, makes friends with several lesser Indian tribes (the Comanche would have fucked him up), and ends up with just two other men from the original crew in Mexico City. He wrote an autobiography about his journey when he was back in Spain. Half of what he writes is complete nonsense, and the other half makes him a celebrity. (Which is what he always wanted: glory) Not one word about me in his entire thousand-page novel, what an asshole!

ON and ON

<u>Hong Kong</u>

One of my favorite things to do is travel. I love seeing new places, interacting with different cultures, and seeing what kinds of adventures are available. I absolutely hate the cold. Do not and will not live in snow ever again. I can afford not to, so I don't. Along those same lines of reasoning, I love summer!! Even hot weather is okay if I can find shade and a cold drink. In the early 1980s (what a great time to be alive.) I had just finished a trip around the world chasing summer. I started in Jordan, hit Australia, the British Islands, Dubai, Peru, Bali, Southern France, Hawaii, the Canary Islands, and Croatia, and finished in San Diego. (Some of those countries now have different names.) I could tell you a different story about the month I spent in each place. Saltwater Croc is hunting in Northern Australia, almost getting jailed in Yugoslavia, many crazy nights in Thailand, eating like a king in Dubai for 10 cents before they found that oil money.

My biggest adventure that year happened at the end of my San Diego, California trip. A small precursor warning. This story has some juvenile male locker-room humor in it. If brothels and strippers offend you, you might wanna skip this chapter and fast forward to the next one.

I was renting a small beach bungalow on Coronado Island. Steps from the beach, enjoying the sunshine and surf. I took my small boat out every morning to catch breakfast and enjoy the sunrise. I had it made, driving around in a loaded CJ5 jeep, looking tan and fit. (As a bonus of whatever it is I have, I never gained weight, I'm a little ashamed to say, but I used a tanning cream because I'm white as fuck), very bit of the eighties' culture shining off of me. I had the Crocket (or Tubbs, I forget which one is Don Johnson's character) haircut rockin'. Banging some Sugar Hill Gang and Run DMC out of my 12-inch subwoofers. I hope you're picking up what I'm putting down; I was living PHAT. I was enjoying the San Diego culture, waves, and nightlife.

One morning, as I returned from my boat, my neighbor Ken stopped me to chat; he was just being social. I liked Ken. He was a stocky, muscular man who wore his long salt-and-pepper hair in a well-kept ponytail. Ken had both arms covered in what I assumed were prison tattoos. His Hispanic features and clothing screamed Mexican mafia. If you saw him, he might seem intimidating; all I cared about was his personality. He was laid back and cool as hell. We had chit-chatted several times. I found him to be easygoing and not a noisy neighbor. We discussed grabbing a beer later that day. I cleaned and prepared the halibut I had caught that morning and decided to take it to Ken's place to share. I am trying to remember what we discussed, but I do remember liking him. It was the beginning of a great friendship. We went from just waving to doing things together. He loved drinking, fishing, surfing, and chasing women. (Just like I did.) Ken didn't seem to have a job, but money wasn't an issue; I figured it was not my business and never asked. He was in his late forties or early fifties. I was in my mid-two thousands. (Perfect fit.) We developed a routine. He'd join me two or three mornings a week to fish.

I'd surf with him whenever I saw him out in the water. We played golf all around southern California. Dinner and *bremelo*s a couple of nights a week. (a *bremelos* is a term for a loose woman, taken from Sir Mix-

A-Lots of the song *Baby Got Back Fame*.) I coulda have also said *Skeezer*. (They are interchangeable) I know I may sound very male chauvinistic, but for most of my life, I have been. No excuses; it was just the way it was. I enjoy the company of women. They are awesome. I never mistreat them. I have loved and married many of them. (Please don't cancel me.)

Ken and I also went to a few Padres games at the Big Q. I Joined a recreational softball team and a pool league. The bottom line is we became real friends. As I said earlier, I typically don't make long-term friends. It's hard to leave them. We were spending at least three days a week together and just doing fun shit.

Ken asked me if I had ever been to TJ. (Tijuana.) Even though it's only a twenty-five-minute drive, I had never made it across the border, so hell yes! I was in. We arrived in TJ just before sunset. Revolution Street is a combination of street food, music, flea markets, excitement, and poverty. Much like every third-world country in the world. Cheap, fun, and dangerous people. We ate bacon-wrapped hot dogs and tacos. Fucking delicious. I had way too many cold beers (as if that's possible.) We walked by and stopped at a few strip clubs.

We inquired about the infamous donkey show. (If you don't know, you don't wanna know what that is.) We never found one. We interacted with some locals, and Ken almost had his expensive watch stolen by a woman who tried to coax us into a lower-end brothel. She grabbed his hand and rubbed it along her tits while expertly undoing his watch band. I had seen this trick done a few times and warned Ken about what was happening. He had no idea and quickly removed his dangling watch from the clutches of her breast. I made fun of him and called him "a pinche gringo" (Ken was one hundred percent not Anglo-Saxon) and also told him, "You look like an easy target. You dressed so nice; roll up your sleeves and show them some of your prison heat!" He smiled at me, and we laughed as we continued up Revolution Street.

We eventually reached what Ken called the "holy grail" of brothels. The *Hong Kong*. It was impressive. Three stories of complete debauchery. A center stage with sexual exploits too far-fetched for you to believe. Shit, I hadn't seen it on display since I was in Asia in the mid-seventeen hundreds. Ken disappeared for almost an hour while I was living the VIP life. I figured he was "tasting the local cuisine." I didn't really miss him. I decided to check out the second and third floors (I am not sure it could get much better). Before I headed up the stairs, I had to shake hands with the man (Piss), and just before I got to the men's room, I caught a glimpse of Ken in a very heated discussion in a booth in the corner.

The music is too loud, and I can't hear what is being said, but there are four very well-dressed Mexican men who look connected from my experiences. (Cartel.) While I'm standing watching, I get greeted by the establishment's muscle and asked very politely to take my gringo ass elsewhere. Ken either knows what he's doing, and this is none of my business, or as a friend, I'm obligated to help. Plus, these fucks don't know I speak Spanish, and their niceties included a few "this pussy and fuck this asshole" mixed in like I wouldn't understand. Just because you say it with a smile doesn't change the fact that I'm being

ON and ON

insulted. So that didn't sit well with me. I mentioned at the beginning that I could fight a little; I also said, "Not professional."

(So, adding up what you know about me. Let's do it together: I can fight, I heal quickly, I haven't died yet, I think I'm smart, I have had at least twelve beers; yea, fuck these *Putos*, aka Bitches! It's on! 'Hang on, Ken, here I come to save you.' Except that's not what happened.)

I *did* knock the first guy out. (Yeah, me!) I immediately made eye contact with Ken, but he didn't return my smile. That's the last thing I remember before waking up in the alley. A nasty bad sanitation, underdeveloped country alley. Ken was sitting next to me. He was beaten to shit too. He told me that when I looked at him, he saw the baseball ball bat swinging at my head. (Fuck, maybe I'm not David Carradine after all.) He was held down and took a small beating. Most of the violence was directed at me. He said I was a tough hombre. We laughed about it on the way back across the border. He couldn't understand how I wasn't more fucked up. "Good genes," I told him. He was even more surprised the following day when I didn't have a scratch, and his face was bruised and swollen. Like any good friend, I called him, he was "a pussy!"

Sometime later, I finally asked him why he was arguing with those men at the bar. He simply said "business," which translates to "none of my fucking *business*." It's not hard to add it all up. Again, let's do it together. Ken doesn't have a nine-to-five job. He has money. He looks the part. Those guys in the booth were Mexican mafia. They didn't kill us (well, him) fuck, Ken's a drug dealer. Armed with those facts, I could have ended our friendship. But why would I do that? It was the 1980s, and everyone did blow!

I had partaken a few times myself. And I'm not the moral police. I did keep a closer eye on my surroundings, and while not snooping, I did notice what I should have seen earlier. A very smoothly run drug operation was being directed by my neighbor Ken. I didn't care. I liked doing all the things we did together. I wasn't lonely. We kept our friendship schedule and hung out even more often. I never brought it up; we never discussed it. He had to have known that I knew. Our relationship continued for another five years or so, basically just being friends. We traveled a few times, and both of us worked through a few short-term girlfriends and just did what friends did.

I first noticed something was up when Ken did not join me fishing for about a week, nor did I see him surfing. I hadn't seen him for about ten days, which was unusual. He had not mentioned going on a trip. I am a big believer in personal privacy (surprised?). Still, I eventually broke into Ken's home and snooped around a bit. What I found was alarming. His house was trashed. It looked like a cop show where they pulled out every drawer, flipped furniture, cut mattresses, and thoroughly ransacked the entire place. No police had been to his house. I would have known if they had been. I had expected some bust for a couple of years because cocaine was being cracked down on all over the country. (*cracked* is funny, but crack wasn't an epidemic yet) Thankfully, I didn't find blood or a missing carpet (too many movies.) I was worried about my friend. But like other friends in the past, I've learned that people make their beds. If the cartel got Ken, I'm sure he deserved it. I had two significant problems. I wasn't a detective, and it had already

ON and ON

been at least ten days. If I was going to do anything to help Ken (if he was still alive and needed my help), I had to act immediately.

I only had one place to start. *Hong* fucking *Kong*!!!! I convinced myself that a little T and A was worth the trip (of course it was.) I was so unconvinced that I would find anything that I brought one hundred, single dollar bills with me. (Better to be prepared.) I drank much less beer this time around. I was completely sober when I arrived at *Hong Kong*. I took a slow walk around the place, making sure to investigate all the secluded booths, and tried not to draw attention to myself. It was as amazing as I remembered. I didn't expect to find Ken sitting at a table feeding dollar bills to a stripper, but somehow, I didn't not expect it either. I did not find him. I also didn't see the cartel guys or any of the bouncers that beat my ass. I'd like to tell you that I left and went straight back to San Diego. Would you believe me? (I didn't think so. Fuck no!) I stayed, met a few San Diego State college rugby players, put every dollar bill I had in spicy little spots, and got drunk as hell. I somehow ended up in an even shittier part of town, miles away from revolution street, missing all my belongings. Fucking strippers! I had no choice but to start my walk of shame back toward the border.

About halfway, I was suddenly bombarded by seven Federales. Someone matching my description had committed some crime. Was there possibly another attractive, lightly shaded red, mostly blond-haired guilty-feeling white guy in TJ? I tried to pay them off with the customary "I can just pay you, and you give it to the judge" standard scheme. Nope. My doppelganger must have done some serious shit. I was arrested and taken to the TJ jail. It was a shit hole but a secure shit hole. I was segregated from the general population; I did not volunteer to speak Spanish. I wanted to hear all the shit being talked about me. It ended up being the usual shit, *stupid white boy, fag, dumb ass being somewhere he shouldn't be.* Quite disappointing. I expected better.

There were about twenty other Caucasian fellas in our own holding cell. Including Ken! I asked, "How and why are you mixed into the cell with all the whites? Did they see that old lady try to steal your watch?"

"Suicide protocol," he said with a smile. Which meant he was suspected as a snitch. He would be shanked (stabbed) if he was among the general population. That sucked, he was in some serious trouble.

I wanted to hug him but refrained due to the current social climate. I told him, "I was undercover looking for you. I had to go on a super classified mission and thoroughly examine the Hong Kong business establishment. I was willing to check every brothel in TJ if that's what it took to find you. My information led me to this particular holding cell." He believed me for about a half second.

His dumb ass got caught trying to cross the border with a hundred pounds of pure Columbian snow. He was going to do some time. Somebody in the bust ring used Ken's info to go on a treasure hunt at his house. Ken told me, "There was nothing there of any value," and was pissed they trashed his place. I agreed to get it all cleaned up and replace whatever was needed. The Mexican Federales caught my look-alike, and I was released four days later. I made my way back to SD and continued to live as usual. I never saw Ken again. He was killed about a year later in his prison cell by cartel members; at least, that's

ON and ON

the rumor. After hearing the news, I packed my shit, got my affairs in order, and bounced. (I always hate losing a friend.)

Looking back at the stories I've told so far, I realized I look like a total dick. The tales are sometimes funny and exciting, but I'm always the hero (of course, I'm the hero; it's my story), and I have shown myself to be a carefree alcoholic and womanizer. I could be in denial, but I don't see myself as either. I can't deny that I love the social aspect and fun of having drinks. I also love women. (Guilty on both counts) I can and have gone years without the company of both, usually not by choice. I was once in a Cambodian prison cell for almost two years. I've been so poor and dirty a woman wouldn't look at me. I've gone through severe lonely depressions where anyone's company was an appalling thought.

I've also been such an egomaniac, and at times, nobody could stand my company. I thought I had grown and matured, but the tales I've told you so far show the opposite. It's a tough thing to open your soul to others and be vulnerable. I will do that now in this following excerpt of my life. (At least try.)

THE TRUTH

I was bouncing around Europe in the mid-1960s. I'm a reader and love news from around the world. I find it very interesting. I was in the habit of starting my mornings outside with a newspaper and a non-alcoholic drink (not coffee, I hate coffee.) I do think the smell of grinding coffee beans is pleasant. Coffee breath is horrendous. I like to enjoy the morning and take in the view or the hustle and bustle of a city. I have come to appreciate the little things in life the most. I will sometimes see a man walking head down hurriedly, going purposely somewhere very important. I then imagine where that destination might be and create a funny or, depending on my mood, a sad story to explain this random person's reason for such haste. People-watching is one of my favorite pastimes.

I was interested in an article about oil exploration in the North Sea. Phillips Petroleum, an American company working in Norway, had shown promising results in finding a sizeable undersea fossil fuel deposit. I'm not a genius, nor can I see the future. Still, I have watched Texas, Saudi Arabia, Argentina, plus many other countries explode with black gold. I had been closely watching where it would happen next, and I wanted a piece of it. The North Sea and Norway could be my ticket.

Since I was in Europe, I traveled to Norway immediately to try to throw some investment money towards this potential jackpot. I didn't want to buy stock; I wanted a small percentage of ownership. It was going to cost me almost everything I had saved. I felt it was worth the risk. (I had been poor before but didn't want to start completely over.)

Arriving in Oslo, I spent a few days checking out the city. Beautiful! It's a wonderfully clean and crisp place. Water everywhere, modern and yet old-world charming. I did touristy things between a couple of business meetings (I got the money rolling.) I took a ferry through the Oslo Fjord and visited a few islands along the way. While visiting a museum dedicated to Viking heritage, I found myself standing next to a woman, both of us looking at a Viking longboat. The boat is unimportant, but the woman became the most important person in my life for the next eighteen years.

She was stunningly gorgeous in a natural beauty way. Long blond hair, pale sparkling blue eyes, athletic, and fit. (Sexy as fuck.) Most importantly, I am single (not for long). She carried herself as if she had no idea how she looked. Carefree but not looking for attention. My first impression was that she knew exactly what she was doing, like Wendy Pfefferkorn from the movie *The Sandlot*. I found out that she had no idea, and she did not care. She was absolutely oblivious to the way she must have made men feel. I didn't throw a pick-up line at her. I asked what she thought about the longboat; she said, "Looks uncomfortable." We shared a small laugh. We walked together from one museum to the next. She accepted my lunch offer, and our conversations continued moving as easily as the Alna River we walked along. I was smitten. She hooked me when she said," See that woman over there; she is in such a hurry. I wonder where she is going?"

I looked at her and said, "She's trying to fit in a quick meeting with her lover before going home to make dinner for her family."

Lisa looked at me and said," You're so dumb." We both laughed. I had not felt an immediate connection like this ever. (Such a different feeling.)

I had come to Oslo for business, but after my afternoon with her, she was all I could think about. I laughed at myself and thought of why this relationship was not a good idea. I say relationship; it had been one afternoon. She had made me work even to get her phone number. I wanted to call her immediately when I returned to my hotel. I wanted to have dinner with her that night. Relationship, what a naive fool. I did call after dinner; my heart raced as the line rang. Her roommate eventually answered and informed me that Sila was out with her boyfriend. (What the FUCK?) Boyfriend? Really? I was dejected. I was heartbroken. I left my hotel information with the roommate and hung up. I felt betrayed. Nothing was ever mentioned about a boyfriend during the five hours we spent together. I collected myself, disappointed and embarrassed by my quick to latch on emotions. Was I being unfair? When was the last time I had been entirely truthful? (Well, never.) Looking logically at the situation, nothing had changed. I met a woman, an extraordinary woman. We enjoyed the day together. (Simple.) I had work to do, and she was just a bonus that I misread.

I was awakened the next morning by a knock at my hotel room door. I answered in my underwear. (It was early.) Sila was standing there looking like a shining ray of sunshine. She smiled and giggled at my appearance. I couldn't help but sheepishly return her smile. Before I invited her in, I wanted answers. I collected myself and sternly said, "Boyfriend?" I was still hurt. My pride was wounded. It was unfair, I had met her yesterday, but I didn't care. I crossed my arms and waited for her answer. "No longer an issue; I choose you." As if I didn't have a choice in the matter. (I didn't.) You might think we needed a long, heartfelt conversation to establish the norms and expectations of our newfound relationship. Nope, that was it. She chose me (I had chosen her standing by the longboat yesterday), and that was it. Done deal.

I loved her immediately. That love grew more profound every day. I threw myself all in for her. She kissed me that morning right after choosing me. It wasn't a passionate 'let's get naked' kiss. It was more of breaking down the barrier between I just met you, but we are on our way to an intimate kiss. She would tell you, "If I didn't kiss him, then he would have been trying all day to pick the right moment."

She was exactly what I didn't know I needed. I had been lonely, but I'd been lonely before; it was more than just a new companion. I very much enjoyed the company of women, but her company was somehow essential. The longer we were together, the more I wanted us to be together. I can't say I needed her with me every second of every day because that would be unhealthy or fair to either of us. I did not want to own her. Her independence is part of the package, which I liked most about her. I eagerly anticipated the moment I would see her next. That feeling of excitement did not change over the years. Even when we would eventually be sharing a bed, waking every morning to her always brought that same level of excitement to me. It wasn't that I felt lucky (I am generally lucky). The feeling I felt was fulfillment. She filled spaces in me that I didn't know needed filling. I had been so closed off emotionally, so private, I had been hiding a big part of myself. (It was like I had a big secret.) I was not ready to expose the truth about myself. The last thing I needed to do was become a lunatic immortal. So I kept that small secret, as always, to myself.

We were inseparable for the next eight days. I would walk Sila home each evening and spend another hour on the phone before bed. On day nine, I woke up to find her naked in my bed. Her skin was light and soft. Her hair reminded me of a warm, safe place (I couldn't resist a Guns and Roses lyric.) She smelled like every best smell mixed together. She was firm and young. (I was just firm!) We took it slow and low, and our fingers explored every inch of each other. The world didn't exist. No words were spoken, and no instructions were needed. The day was spent in my hotel room. It was the best day of my long life.

We talked for hours and discussed our dreams and our personal histories. I didn't lie; I couldn't tell the whole truth. I grew up on a farm, and my family was killed in a fire. I was only twenty-two, so I had to leave out and hide several of the skills I had acquired. It was easiest to explain being able to build things. Believable that I sold the farm and made a few smart investments. Having money just made "life a little easier," I told her, and it was the reason that had brought me to Oslo. Of course, I left out sailing, rum running, road building, Indian chasing, and not dying. I also didn't mention being sterile. It was never an issue until it was a huge issue a couple of years later. Sila was determined to finish her studies at Oslo University. Family was a big part of her life. I was excited to meet her parents. She made it clear to me that she wanted a big family with several children. (A big problem to be dealt with later.) As much as I could justify the things I didn't tell her, they would eventually create a hole between us that only the truth would fill.

We continued our romance. Over the next year, Sila graduated, I met her parents (more on them later), and I bought a fixer-upper house just outside of Oslo. My investment in the North Sea was still looking promising. We worked on the house together. I poured my heart and soul into the house and Sila. While she painted, tiled, or picked color schemes, the light in her eyes is etched into my memories. There was an unsaid agreement that this was our house.

We took short three five -to five-day trips together as any couple in love would do. One of my favorite trips was to a small Mexican town on the Baja Peninsula called Cabo San Lucas. The coastal desert landscape makes it one of my favorite places in the world. Great seafood and cold Mexican beers add to the allure. Cabo would eventually attract the attention of large hotel chains and resort builders. It would become a place for celebrities, athletes, and millionaires. (I kick myself for not buying a small piece of land.) In the late 1960s, Cabo was still a hidden treasure of a small fishing village. We rode motorcycles around the Baja Peninsula and had dinner one night in the nearby town of Todos Santos. The Hotel California from the band The Eagles is located in Todos Santos. The hotel is claimed to be haunted, but I didn't see any signs of it. (Thank God, you know that shit creeps me out!) The locals were terrific; we were directed to a hidden beach with a long, shallow surf break. It's perfect for beginner surfers. We borrowed a couple of surfboards and, without instruction, attempted to surf. The water was perfect, the waves rolled in, and I.....had so much trouble catching a wave (complete bullshit!) Sila had no problem at all. She was up riding the waves while I struggled. I did eventually catch on and we had an unforgettable day. Her athleticism was amazing. I would toss items to her. Keys, items from the market, fruits, you name it, she would quickly, without effort, catch everything. We threw a newly invented toy, a flying disc called a frisbee, to each other on the beach. Everyone knows what a frisbee is today, but it was very new in the 1960s. Around the time I was on the chain gang in France, anyone with a frisbee would have been burned at the stake for consorting with the devil. I only mention the frisbee because Sila had trouble throwing it. I could sling that little flat disc, but she couldn't do it. (Finally got her.)

We chartered a boat early one morning and set sail for a day of fishing. The waters of the Sea of Cortez are teaming with sea life. Our target that day was blue marlin. We hooked into three and landed two; Sila, I'm ashamed to say, bagged both. I did catch a few dorados; we BBQed those and fresh lobster that evening on the sand while watching the sunset. It was perfect. I didn't have a ring (well, not an engagement ring), but I proposed to her right there on the beach that night. (Luckily, I didn't have a ring; I might have tossed it to her.) When she excitedly said, "Of course, I will marry you," I was as happy as I've ever been. I had picked the right moment. Thank God, she chose me.

Sila's family was very close. Her dad was a tall, bushy-haired man. He was talkative and personal. He was a photographer but also very artsy. He loved motorsports and would travel worldwide to take pictures at race events. He had been to America several times but also to Australia and France. He loved nature, was a bird watcher, and was a member of several philanthropic organizations. Everyone in Oslo knew him personally or by reputation. He was very protective of his only daughter. It took a little while for him to warm up to me, but he eventually did. He once invited me on a four-day hike. I met some of his friends and explored The Scandinavian Coastal Forest. Impressive, to say the least. As we walked on the second day together, he asked about my intentions with his daughter. I told him I loved her; I had never met anyone like her, and with his permission, I would ask her to marry me. We continued to walk without a response from him. When the trip was over, he looked at me after everyone else had left. He said, "If you're fortunate enough that she will have you, then you have my blessing." but he added, "You will have to talk to her mother as well." and "Good luck with her." I found it strange, but I was willing to do whatever was needed.

Sila's mom was incredible. I can't even begin to explain this spectacular person. She was warm, loving, kind, giving, and fun. She was full of energy. Loved hosting a party and loved to laugh. She was also very naive. She saw the best in people, and I never heard her curse. She was genuinely a unique soul. It was almost too easy to play a practical joke on her. Once, I brought a rubber snake to their house. It was semi-life-like. Any look longer than three seconds, and it was easy to tell it was clearly fake. Sila put it next to her mom on the couch where they were sitting; it scared the shit out of her. Ok, it's mean but funny. Even funnier was when we put the same fake ass snake by her shoes, and it scared the shit out of her again. It was as if it was the first time she had seen it. Then, in the ice box. Then, on her pillow. Finally, in a puzzle box. Same reaction every time, fucking classic! When we weren't teasing her, we played cards together. Sundays were for family. I missed very few Sundays. It was always a great meal followed by an intense session of whist (a pinochle-ish game) or bridge. I got my ass kicked every Sunday.

I firmly believe Sila's mom somehow knew that I was missing a motherly figure. Even before she was told my parents were killed in a fire, she encompassed me in love. She always had something for me, as simple as freshly baked cookies or as unwanted as advice. (She was mostly right.) She seemed to know me inside and out. (Apple doesn't fall from the tree.) I can say without hesitation that I dearly loved her. I would do anything for her, and there was always something she could find for me to do. I readily answered every call, no matter the time of day or what I was doing. I had no problem dropping any and everything to help her. She became my mom. Funny how God works.

I didn't expect any issues asking her permission to marry Sila. In hindsight, I should have expected the list to be pulled from her pocket and the interview that followed. Her dad gave me an easy two-day silence; her mom gave me a thought-out twenty-question interrogation in a lovely, put-me-on-the-spot-with-nowhere-to-run manner. I was cornered. She was very personal. Questions ranged from my sexual satisfaction, duties that I expected from my wife and children, what I thought being a father meant, and whether I loved her daughter. I answered everything truthfully, even admitting to premarital sex with her daughter. (Sila had already spilled the tea to her.) If I were being recorded, it would be a great episode of the TV show *Punked*. I must have passed because she stood up and hugged me tightly, saying," I know you'll do great; I love you." Permission granted.

ON and ON

We were married on a clear, warm day in September. Sila was stunningly beautiful as ever. The ceremony was small and personal. The honeymoon was short and very personal. Sila wanted babies. I felt terrible, and I was more than willing and excited to perform the baby-making process. She would be utterly disappointed each month when it was settled that no babies were fertilized. She blamed herself and tried every wife's tale to help the process. We did it in the mornings, we did it after lunch, and we were always doing it. After two years, I told her it had to be me. Fertility clinics and in vitro were still a decade or so away. I asked if she could still be happy without children. She said, "She didn't know." Of course, I was crushed. My maturity kicked in here; I would have disappeared in previous relationships. This time, I refused to leave her (or her mom.)

The house had long since been finished, and the North Sea had provided one of the largest petroleum deposits ever discovered. I had enough money for several more lifetimes. What if we took an extended vacation to see the world together? Sila said, "She would trade every drop of oil in that damn sea for one child." Later, she would say, "What good is a house with no family in it." An emptiness was growing between us. We both felt it. She was unhappy, and I couldn't fix it. She couldn't understand why I wasn't as upset as she was. "didn't I want to be a father?" I already knew it wasn't in my cards. She was still hoping to catch the one card needed for the straight. (Poker reference.)

Adoption was an option for us. Sila said, "she'd consider it." In the meantime, we continued to live, travel, and make love. All were good and mostly great. We had many fun adventures together. Things became routine but in a good, comfortable way. We continued to try for children for another five years. Waking every morning to her next to me in our bed is something I did not take for granted. One morning, she looked at me and said, "We need to talk." Her stone-cold seriousness made my heart stop. She spoke in a matter-of-fact way that chilled me. "There is something you are not telling me; I know you have secrets that you are not telling me. I want them all, everything!"

I used my usual "What are you talking about?" "I'm with you every day."

She said, "When did you learn to speak French?" Then she said, "Show me your leg where you cut it yesterday when you stepped off the wall in the backyard."

"French? When did I speak French?"

"Stop fucking bullshitting me; I heard you on the phone yesterday with some fool about your oil shit!"

I was stuck. How much would Sila believe? What was enough? I knew the gap between us was widening; would the whole truth be too much? I decided to explain everything, leaving nothing out. I would give her an overview and then answer any questions after.

I asked her to get dressed, and I would tell and show her things about me that I had kept from her. We sat at our kitchen table, and I began. First, I spoke in English (our everyday language), then switched to Norwegian (also called Bokmal). She spoke this language too, and then, in quick succession, I went from German to French, Portuguese, Spanish to Latin, to Scottish. She said nothing. I asked, "Is that enough because know a few more?"

ON and ON

"How?" was all she asked.

"That is the part I'm not sure you're ready for," I replied. She sat staring at me. Stone-faced, but I saw an inquiring, investigative crinkle developing around her body. Like when she is working on a jigsaw puzzle. I looked into her scared eyes and said, "What I'm going to tell you is unbelievable; it will sound made up. I have no reason to lie. It will be tough to believe. You cannot tell anyone, EVER!" I made her swear to keep my secret; I promised her I wasn't in trouble. I wasn't a fugitive; no one was hunting me. I wasn't a criminal or sexual predator. I had been vague about my past with her, but I was going to throw the whole shit show at her at once.

The first thing I did was pull down my sock where there should have been a big fresh wound or a new scab. I told her I heal very quickly. I walked to the counter, took a knife from the block, and ran it across my palm. A nice deep gash appeared and bled some. I made her look at it to acknowledge the crazy man had cut himself. I then closed my palm, waited about 1 minute, and showed her my hand, which now only had a light red line. No gash, no blood, soon to, be no evidence of a cut. "How? Why have I never noticed?" she asked.

I told her, "I am very good at covering my injuries." I added, "I've had years to perfect it." I continued, "I have shown you what your eyes can see, and your ears can hear. Do you believe I can speak several languages and heal remarkably quickly?" She nodded in agreement. "What I'm going to tell you now, you will either believe or not. I can only prove it with more words. I don't have physical proof." I waited for her to try to grasp what was happening. I needed her to categorize in her mind what she had just witnessed to allow room for the bigger, harder to believe, rest of the story.

"I was 22 years old when I died. I've had several near-death experiences since. Otherwise, I'm an average guy. Not a genius, no photographic memory. I do read people's body language extremely well, but that's more of a learned skill. I can fight but not great, can shoot but not a marksman, can speak several languages, you have witnessed it, athletic but not a pro. I am good at most athletic activities, except surfing," I added, looking for a smile I hadn't received. I took a deep breath and continued, "I love to sing but cannot play an instrument. I think I'm hilarious. I'm self-sufficient. I can cook and build shit." This is how I started.

"What do you mean you were 22 when you died? You were 22 when I met you, and we have been together for over eight years. Are you saying you're a fucking ghost?" was her reply.

"Far from a ghost, I'm afraid of ghosts, you know this," I smiled. Again, she didn't return it. "I don't age, I don't have one scar on my body, so far, I've been alive more than two thousand years."

Sila stood up and walked away. She left the house and did not return the entire day. I was left alone to ponder my mistake. Why would I tell her? I had just fucked up the best thing that ever happened to me. Sure, I would survive; I always did. The loss of Sila somehow felt deeper. It was going to hurt more than leaving other lives. Hurt more than those arrows the Comanche shot me with? Most definitely. I prayed she would come back. I owed her as long as it took, even if she never wanted to see me again.

ON and ON

She did return and surprised me by saying, "We are adopting a baby! I've been at the agency all afternoon." She added, almost in passing, "I do have questions; I will get to them in time. Time seems to be the one thing you have in abundance."

It still makes me smirk that I worried Sila wouldn't be Sila in every colossal moment. I had taken an enormous risk in revealing myself; she proved her love to me by not only believing but believing in a way only she possibly could. She was determined to live by her vows even if her husband was a deranged, lunatic, crazy mother fucker. More questions ensued in the following days, months, and years. The first question cut right through the bullshit to the bone. "So.....two thousand years, huh? How many other wives?"

(Well fuck.) "Twelve." was my answer.

"Less than one per hundred years? Seems off." Sila questioned with her arms crossed. "I'd expect more; I would have had a new man about every fifty to sixty years."

"I needed breaks, and I wasn't always as established as I am today."

"Never fathered a child?"

"Never."

"Name your wives in order."

I did without hesitation or pause. While she stared through me, Sila said, "ok, I'm not jealous. I feel the way you love me; it pours out of you. I'm not saying I understand or completely believe everything you have told me. But I believe that you believe it. That's enough for me as of right now. You have the rest of my life to convince me. Let's go to the bedroom."

Our nightly routine became me telling the stories I'm writing now to her. She loved them. She would inquire about details much more profound than I'm telling you. I skipped over past lovers (no one wants to hear that shit.) She always had a "Why were you there?" or "Really? You were such an ass." She loved being spoken to in the many languages I knew. Sila laughed so hard about Da Vinci. Marveled at my tells of the Azores, was pissed about buying enslaved people, and couldn't believe I was scalped or that I befriended a child molester. She insisted I make wine and wanted to hear more about meeting Diego again. She was also very interested in the origins of my ring. She was slowly really beginning to believe everything. Our life together without secrets opened me up to become someone entirely new. It was transitional. I wasn't always guarded. I was no longer angry. One day, I woke up, and that small rise-up knot in my soul was no longer there; it felt as if I wouldn't be able to get mad no matter how hard I tried.

Exactly one year after my tell-all. We brought our little bundle of joy home. She wasn't exactly a baby. She was almost two years old. She was a spark plug with curly strawberry-blond hair and light green eyes. We were told by the adoption agency that she might need some time to adjust to us. We required the adjustment time. She was a thousand miles an hour with an inquisitive mind who needed to explore everything. She had to touch everything, put everything in her mouth, and just as quickly disregard those items in the wake of destruction. Chairs had to be placed on top of tables so she wouldn't climb on top of those tables. Once, I found her standing on the stove, looking out

ON and ON

the window at a pair of nesting birds. There was no obstacle too high nor an item not worth checking out.

When she slept, it was as if someone had turned off a light switch, but mostly, that light was always on and blazing. She was eager to hug and deliver kisses but just as anxious to squirm out of your arms and bolt to her next adventure. She loved cuddling up with me and falling asleep. I took many impromptu naps with her. We named her Elsa, my little Elsy. She brought a light into our home and lives. I took her everywhere with me. I was, for the first time, a proud father. As everyone with a child knows, your love for that child completely differs from other loves you have known. I was responsible for this little person, me! (And Sila too, I guess.)

As she grew, she was fearless. She rode her two-wheeler bike before she was four and refused training wheels. "Those were for babies, "she exclaimed forcibly. I was on skis at three, flying down hills. (She was adorable in her little snow hat.) I even bought her a little dirt bike when she was five. She was my shadow. We worked in the garden together, went fishing in my boat (of course, she drove), did our chores, fed the animals, played jokes on Grandma, and spent time with Mom. Now, I was complete.

To say I spoiled her wouldn't be entirely accurate. She didn't get everything she wanted. We taught her to save and work. She had chores. We taught her that no one gets a free ride in this life. We were strict about her schoolwork and taught her to be respectful of others. She went to fundraisers and helped her grandfather at charitable events. When she was young, I spoke to her in multiple languages, and she picked them up quickly. Of course, there were incidences of youthful defiance. (I would have worried if there wasn't.) She made friends quickly, and there were always two or three extra girls for sleepovers and campouts, the usual day-to-day shit.

I hope I am expressing the absolute joy Elsy brought me. Combining that joy with the love Sila soaked me in and having an extended family who I cherished, I could not have been happier. I was never or ever again so blessed.

The weather in Oslo can be extreme. Beautiful, warm summers give way to stunning winter snows. It gets cold; I told you earlier I hated the cold, and it's true. Sila's parents would not leave Oslo; therefore, I endured the cold winter months. I pulled everyone away for a few weeks yearly to a much warmer climate. Mexico was a favorite; we also traveled to Ecuador, the Bahamas, and even the Azores, plus several other less frigid climates. Our family vacations always included my in-laws; I wouldn't have it any other way. Driving home from the airport on a colder-than-normal snowy night, we were exhausted from our long flight back from Fiji. The airport was only a half-hour drive from home. I was careful on the icy roads and drove exceptionally cautiously. I wish every driver on the road that night was as cautious as I was. The road to our house was a single-lane street.

A man driving a truck loaded with long trees to make telephone poles was driving as cautiously as me. The young teenage boy driving his father's truck was not. He passed the larger tree truck going way too fast, lost control, and flipped his truck head-on into us. It happened in

ON and ON

an instant. I slammed on my brakes, but black ice caused us to skid as if two magnets were attracted together.

I awoke in an ambulance. I forced my way outside. The scene was total destruction, with car parts and body parts everywhere. I stood barefoot and shirtless, looking at the complete annihilation of my perfect life. Every person in every vehicle involved in the accident was dead. (Except for me, of course.) I wish I was killed also. I did die inside. I cannot go into more detail about the crash site. It hurts too much.

Everything I cherished was gone in an instant. One more minute at the luggage carousel, if I had waited longer to turn out of the airport parking lot, taken an earlier or later flight, drove one mile an hour faster or slower. I wanted it to be my fault. I wanted to take the blame. Maybe God was tired of my found happiness. (I know that is not true.) I never have nor will believe that *everything happens for a reason*; that is just complete bullshit! There is no explainable reason why everyone I loved was stolen from me. It is just life! And life can fucking suck!

I cannot say it changed me in a good way. Sila and Elsy could still be alive today. I could still be living my best-loving life. They showed me that genuine, unselfish love can untie every knot, expose and accept every lie, and harvest every dead soul. My fake, always making a joke, drinking too much, keeping everything inside, and fearing sharing the true me was opened up. It did not happen all at once. (I couldn't just write a story about the true me yet) I did learn a lot about life and how to live it better. After a few years of total self-destruction and few thousand "don't give a fuck about anything," I realized that life is much more than adventures, socially good times, and cheap sex. (All those can be fun, and I recommend them in moderation.) There must be a purpose, something more. Sila showed it to me. Elsy hammered it home. I wasn't ready for it after they left me. I had to mourn; I had to re-remember it. I went back to my old ways. (Two thousand years will make you a little stubborn.) Their love lessons slowly seeped out of me. Just a little at a time over twenty or so years. (Not that long of a time comparatively.) I was a better friend to Ken than to Jehon, Alfredo, or Da-vid. I still can't imagine loving again. That hurts way too much. I am still very guarded. I did, however, open up and share a piece of myself with you. A very personal, intimate secret about me: plus, I'm writing this book. Sila and Elsy would be proud of me. (A little disappointed in me too.) That's fucking personal growth!

There is not a day that I don't think about that time in my life. Simple things like washing dishes bring back vivid memories of our house. A child laughing. A family riding bikes together. I could go on and on. It's been over fifty years since I last saw Sila and Elsy. I see them daily in my thoughts and every night in my dreams.

ON and ON

<u>Jareth</u>

I almost died once before that Roman blade ultimately opened my eyes to who I am. I was maybe twelve, and Jareth was ten. We were not quite old enough to have real jobs on the farm, just daily chores. Our days always started before dawn. There were cows to milk and animals to feed. The plowing and other adult jobs would be a couple of years away for both of us. If we could get our chores done quickly enough and avoid our parents, who could always find more work for us, we would have the whole day to do whatever we liked. We like to fish and hunt and explore. We would discuss plans the night before.

"We could hike to the River Conon, fish until late afternoon, and bring home dinner." Jareth started as soon as we were in bed.

"You always want to fish. Let's go explore Smoo Cave." I tried to convince him.

"You just want to see the Dunbar girls. You know if we get caught, their dad will lash us with his whip."

"He might catch you; that ol' fecker will never set his hands upon me."

"So, I get whipped so you can make funny eyes at some girls? Go by yourself to the caves. I don't like them anyway. You always make me go inside too far. They are off limits; Ma and Dad say so."

"Fine, scary pants. Let's fish, but whoever catches the biggest the other does the fish cleaning."

After chores the next morning, we set off on the roughly three-mile hike to the River Conon. It was a cloudy, overcast day, like most days in Scotland. The sun peaks through for moments but hides away most of the day. We walk and throw stones at rabbits. I pretend to see bear scat to scar Jareth. He was always so gullible. As I laugh at his more and more clearly afraid questions, we top the hill and see the river below. This changes his demeanor, and we both run down the hill, excited to be the first to find the right stick and attach our yarn and bone hook. (How we caught a fish with those rigs is crazy, but we did.)

Jareth had more patience than I did. He would scan the river to look where he thought the fish might be and stay in one spot for hours. I roamed up and down and across the river, taking the bait in multiple places for minutes. I thought, "If the fish are hungry, I'll bring dinner to them."

Jareth would laugh and say, "You have to sneak up on them and not show them you are there."

We fished for several hours, and I had a couple of nice sea trout, but nothing huge. I hadn't seen Jareth for a while as I wandered the river. I knew he'd be in the same spot or very close to it. He was looking at me with a massive smile as I walked up to him. He reached down and pulled a giant, at least thirty-pound salmon, from the grass by his feet.

Holy hell," I exclaimed excitedly, running now to get a closer look at it.

Looks like you'll be cleaning today," he smugly replied.

I had to clean ten fish, but only three were my catch. Usually, I might have tried to renege on our deal, but that salmon was something special. We might be in a bit of trouble for sneaking off, but bringing home such a meal was our get outta jail free card. He gave me every detail of catching it while I gutted and cleaned.

"It came from nowhere and attacked my bait; it hit it so hard I almost dropped my pole. I was sure it was going to break the yarn. Don't know how I managed to land it."

"Amazing," I said, looking up at him. My enjoyment was immediately halted. "Jareth," I told as calmly as possible. "Please don't turn around; just walk slowly past me."

"What? Why are you so serious? Why are you talking so quiet and funny?"

"There are two bear cubs behind you."

He looked at me and laughed, "Do you ever stop? Why are you always trying to scare me?"

I dropped the knife, and the fish grabbed him and pulled him with me in the opposite direction.

"Run!" I yelled. He started running with me, but his curiosity superseded his fear, and he turned to look back. His foot hit a rock, and he skidded in the river. I grabbed his shirt to pull him up, and with both of us knee-deep in the river, we watched as momma bear bounded towards us. She stopped two feet in front of us. She stood on her hind legs and was seven or eight feet tall. Spit covered our faces as she roared an ear-splitting warning at us. I turned and pushed Jareth into the river's current. Picked up a hand-sized stone from the water and flung it at her. She hit me with her paw and knocked me four or five feet into the water; she was on top of me before I could get my face to the surface for a breath. My vision was blurring, my breath was escaping bubbles, and both her front paws covered my face.

Jareth says, "She just stopped as if she was bored of killing you. She just turned and left. Walked over and stole my salmon and guided her cubs away." I was face down in the river, blood everywhere. Jareth dragged me to shore and carried me over his shoulder into the grass. The up and down from his walking must have acted as some Heimlich maneuver and pushed water from my lungs. I began to cough as he laid me down. I had deep gashes on both shoulders but no bite wounds. She hit me and held me underwater. I had broken ribs and a concussion. I was most likely in shock, too. Jareth made a fire and a quick shelter. He cleaned my shoulder injuries, and I slept through what must have been a very long, cold night for him. The next morning, he carried me the long three-mile hike home over his ten-year-old shoulder. I vaguely remember the trip. He would mention it for the next ten years whenever he needed something from me. I think the trip eventually got to be over ten miles long when he told the story. I recovered quickly. (Not like now.) I would have died that day if Jareth wasn't with me. I also would not have gone fishing that day; I would have been alone in a cave with one of the Dunbar girls.

ON and ON

Cheating, Sniping, and Gold

I was alone again in London in 1890-ish. I had just left Spain in a huge hurry, just before the police could charge me with arson (and impersonating myself.) I was claiming to be my own son. I had a land claim from forty years earlier, and the land that was rightfully mine had been stolen from me by……. wait for it…….the fucking church! I argued for several months until I was told to leave or face charges. I learned several times that it's better to leave the church alone, but again, I'm a slow learner and stupidly stubborn. The land was mine; I had all the correct paperwork. The church had taken the land and grew a marvelous grape vineyard. The vineyard had been growing for almost thirty years. The wine was excellent and a giant cash cow for the church.

I was asked to donate the land to "help the poor." When I refused, even at the expense of damning my soul, the clergy just decided to keep it. I was pissed; I had planned to sell that property for a nice profit. Instead of leaving like a good little peasant, I set fire to the entire place, the church included. (Sinful!) After watching a gigantic bonfire, I rode without sleep for almost a week. (I did keep the deed to the land; maybe it could still be useful.) I finished my journey in London with enough money to hold me over and no real need for employment.

I had a long trip to decide my next move or scheme, depending on your character level. I bet you can guess where this is going. I went straight to a racetrack to recruit a few men who had both the connections needed and who wanted to make a quick buck. After a few days, I thought I had found both. I checked two of the biggest tracks in London. The first track was called Chester Racecourse, commonly known as the Roodee. It is still in operation today. It is the longest standing race track in the world. The second trace was Alexandra Park; this course lasted a little over a hundred years but shut down in the 1970s.

I watched who oversaw loading the horses into the gate. I narrowed it down between two men. Scotty was a well-dressed, all-business, bowlegged, clean-shaven tall man who always wore a cloth cap that snapped in the front. He wore glasses and had a sizeable British nose with a few nose hairs always sticking out. He also had no chin. (It must have been a quick shave.) I spoke to him in passing a few separate times to become familiar with each other, at least to look familiar; I pretended to be chummy by using his name. "Hey Scotty, great job today; we all appreciate you getting them all in on time." The next day, it was, "Scotty, see you at the pub after? Your first one is on me, mate." Shit like that. Scotty was a man who was by the books and took real pride in his job. The other fella, Leo, was not as professional. He was very pale, much shorter, and always seemed dirty. He would yell and scream at his co-workers. Whenever I saw him, he wore the same dirty-ass brown tweed coat, and his hair and beard were untidy. When I tried to make the same small talk to Leo, he replied, "Feck off!!" followed by a harsh, unrecognizable insult in a thick iron curtain accent. I concluded that he was Russian and connected to organized crime.

I followed Scotty after the track closed on two separate occasions. Both times, he went straight to his tiny flat with a perfectly manicured

ON and ON

lawn and garden. I waited a few hours each time to see if he ventured elsewhere, but he didn't.

When I followed Leo, however, he went straight to a local pub filled with men who looked as dirty and mean as he did. The pub had a reputation as a place you should avoid unless you looked like they did. Rough and Russian. I was neither, and I would have stood out like a dick on a wedding cake. It was impossible to approach Leo without creating the proverbial record scratch. Instead, I waited until he walked out alone and tried to be friendly. Leo brushed me off and said, "Leave me alone, you bloody queer!" Pointing a sharp-looking knife at me. I held up my hands and said, "I am inquiring if you were open to a business deal that is in no way sexual."

"I don't know you; I don't do business with people I don't know."

"I could buy you a pint and tell you about my idea."

He thought about it for a short while, then said, "Fek off, like I told ye two days ago, and do not follow or approach me again, or I will shove this blade up your pasty arse!" He then turned and walked away. He had called me both pasty and gay; I took no offense to either; I knew I was neither. I'm unsure if my maturity or the thought of that rusty blade made his insults not bother me. (You know, it bothered me.) Leo was a dead end. I thought he would be perfect, but he refused to speak to me. He was either very connected or terrified of someone. (My guess is both.)

With no other alternative, I followed Scotty. I spoke to him every day during that week. It had gotten to the point where he was acknowledging me before I talked to him. There was no change in his routine for another week before he finally veered away from his flat after work. I saw Mr. Straight and Narrow entering a bakery. I waited around a corner and walked by him as he exited. "Hey, Scotty!" I exclaimed.

"Great to see you; what brings you around here?"

"Needed a few loaves, I'm so sorry, but I forgot your name; I was going to ask you yesterday."

"Not a problem. It's Greg, "I manufactured. "I'm headed for a quick pint before I head home to the misses, my treat, if you have the time?"

"Maybe later in the week, gotta get back."

"No worries, I'm going to hold you to it; we need to catch up."

I left it at that. My first claw was in. Patience was a quality I had in excess.

Over the next two months, I persuaded Scotty to finally join me at the pub. He drank very slowly, was very pleasant, and liked gossiping about the track affairs. We became friends, well, kinda friends. I was using him and felt a little bad about it. I promised myself it would be worth it to Scotty in the end. I danced around topics of cheating at the racetrack. "Has anyone ever gotten caught cheating at the track?" I finally asked him.

"Not as often as you might think; one bloke tried to pass off counterfeit money once." was his easy reply. "I've heard tales of doped-up ponies and rumors of fixed races, but only rumors. I stay away from those things. Mr. Flanigan, the track owner, deals with that sort of business." He added as he looked around, checking for eavesdroppers.

ON and ON

Mr. (Franklin) Flanigan was a handsome, fit-looking man. He wasn't extremely large, but not small either. He had a gray full head of hair and a handlebar mustache, which was also gray. He had taken the track away from the previous family of owners more than ten years ago through brutality and blackmail. He was a mean fuck, with a charming outer shell. A salesman of smiles but a venomous serpent. A man who would hold your infant child lovingly while explaining the details of why you were signing your business over to him. He was always expensively sharp dressed. A non-Royal dressed as a Royal. He was the most powerful criminal in London. Mr. Flanigan had staved off a few hostile takeovers from the Irish and the Armenian mobs in recent years. The stories I was told included hundreds of bodies and extreme brutality. A man not to be fucked with, Scotty was petrified of him. (Me, a little less.)

Scotty then surprised me by saying, "I've been waiting a month to hear your proposal; what do you have in mind, *Greg*?"

Getting caught in my lie, I almost denied my intentions. "What? I would never!" was what my first instinct was to say. Instead, I took a moment, looked him right in the eyes, and said,

"Money, lots of money."

The Scotty, who lives in his tidy, well-maintained flat that rarely ventures out in the world, was not the man sitting across the table from me. While I was trying to con him, he had been fooling the world as a whole.

Scotty stared intensely at me and quietly said, "I spend every evening in my house thinking of ways to get out of here; I have drawn up elaborate plans to hit a big-time score. What I lack is you."

"My plan is not to win once and run away," I told him. "Greed and stupidity will get you caught and killed."

"A long-term skim or scheme will be noticed and get me caught and killed as well." Scotty calmly retorted.

I dug into my memories from long ago. I could now tell him what me and my brother had learned from Sly. "Past posting on a medium to long shot, a couple of smaller unnoticed wagers, then one last big bet after a couple of medium losses," I explained.

He just stared at me and closed his eyes, thinking. Running the plan through his mind. His fingers were rubbing against themselves like right before you wanted to grab something hot.

"Place a small wager on a long shot, win, then place a bigger bet on another long shot and lose. Then, try to recapture or chase with another much larger bet on an even bigger underdog. All using the same betting station to show what a degenerate gambler I am."

"Exactly!" I proclaimed.

"It's simple and practical; I should have thought of it myself," he replied.

"We will need to find a fast, unknown, unremarkable horse. You will have to quietly slide that horse into the gate only twice, so the risk is less. You also need an exit plan to leave quickly after collecting the last score.

ON and ON

"I've been working on my exit route for over five years. I know where I want to go. I know how to get there. I couldn't figure out how to appropriate the money to make it happen. I sit in my flat drawing up wild plans to collect the money I need to leave this awful city." He paused as the gears of his mind tumbled along, "I know a couple of breeding stables where we might locate the steed we need. I'll need a few pounds to grease a few fingers. Getting the horse into the proper gate will not be a problem." Scotty confidently replied.

With the plan in motion, that just left my exit plan. After collecting my money. I would go to Paris and then catch a train to Turkey. I had pondered my next adventure over the last month. I would need to get far away from London but in small increments. A ship would be too boxy if someone happened to follow me. A train would work best. I could exit any town along the way if I felt any danger. The railway passage I would take would become very famous after Agatha Christie wrote a mystery novel called *The Orient Express.*

Scotty was prohibited from gambling at the track, but he found an off-track betting site to place the first wager. I used a betting station at the track. The first race we bet went smoothly, and we collected a nice sum without anything but a "well-done sir" from the betting station attendant. We waited ten days before placing the second bet. I had been calculating the shift rotations to be sure the same attendant was working the booth.

"Hopefully, lightning will strike twice," I told him as I placed my next wager on a medium-odds horse.

I have never been less happy to collect money when our second horse won. "Feking blind luck."

Scotty laughed that evening over a pint.

The plan had to be rescheduled due to my train departure in Paris. It was a monthly route. The last thing I wanted was to be anywhere near London or even Paris after stealing Franklin Flanigan's money.

"You should sell betting tips on long shot ponies," the betting attendant told me as I collected the winnings from my third long shot winnings in a row. "I could pass the word around if you like. What's your name mate?"

I replied, "No thanks."

Winning was the absolute last thing we needed. We would have to lose and lose a few in a row. There was already too much attention on me. I knew it would happen, and it didn't surprise me when two large, greasy men approached me as I walked into the track a few days later. Both men were heavy-set with slicked-back dark hair.

"Er, he is the magic man," Heckle said to Jeckle.

"Got a keen eye for the ponies; dis one does," Jeckle added.

I stood silently and just stared at them. Both stood so I could see the pistols in their waistbands. Fucking with these guys was not an option.

"Mr. Flanigan has revoked your guess past Piss off."

"And don't come back."

I nodded my head, turned, and walked out of the stadium grounds. How the hell could I be so lucky? Fortunately, Scotty had not run into

ON and ON

the same trouble. He collected his winnings and still had the venue to place more bets. The easy workaround for my problem was betting through a proxy. Over a thousand years later, I had to find a trustworthy drunk. (That's a myth, like a pink unicorn or a pot of gold at the end of a rainbow.) I didn't want a repeat of Jareth and me beating that old guy's ass, so instead, I asked the bartender at the pub I had been frequenting if he was willing to place a couple of bets for me. "I won three longshot bets, and now they no longer want my business," I complained as his shift ended. "I'll make it worth your efforts; I'll pay you a month's salary to place two bets for me. Upfront today if you like. The first bet will lose, and the second bet will win. Guaranteed!"

I again go back to the old saying, "Money talks and bullshit walks." Money did the talking. The bartender was happy to collect an extra month's salary for placing my two bets, and we set the plan in motion. "The second bet will be substantial," I told him. "Bring a couple of friends with you when you collect."

I paid and told him, "I'll give you the money for the second bet eight days from today." He didn't say much. Took the money and repeated what was to be done and which horse he would bet on the following day. Thankfully, I finally lost. My horse came in last place at twenty-five to one. (Which pays zero money.)

Eight days later, I met Jimmy and the bartender at a different pub several miles from the race track. We had over two hours before race time to ensure everything was perfectly set in motion. Scotty had determined the best race to bet, and I gave Jimmy the info and money.

It would be an extensive collection. I had my exit route confirmed. I was ready to roll.

You may find this hard to believe, but I didn't fully trust Jimmy. I followed him to the track but stayed far enough to not be spotted by Jimmy or any of Franklin Flanigan's men. If Jimmy would have tried to steal my money, I don't know what I would have done. I was at his mercy. I was looking in the wrong direction. Jimmy had no intention of stealing from me. He was just greedier than I anticipated. Jimmy placed my bet as agreed upon. He also had one of his mates place a bet using all the month's salary I gave him earlier. (I had told him it was a guaranteed win. I wonder why I was surprised he placed his bet.)

Me and Scotty had talked at length about the right amount to bet to not raise too many suspicions. I just wanted enough money to hold me over and make a fresh start elsewhere. Scotty had some savings and just wanted an escape. I had told Scotty to pick a different betting station, "I know these blokes; I'll be just fine." was his answer. "You worry too much; no one will miss the small amount of the big pie the track collects daily. People do win; it is already calculated into their formula."

Our pony won its race at forty to one. Jimmy's winnings, combined with ours, threw red flags everywhere. Our winnings alone would have led to an investigation. Combine Jimmy's extra bet with it, and the officials at the track must have gone crazy. Our scheme would be eventually figured out. I just wanted a day or two head start before they came looking for us. It took less than thirty minutes for the dogs to be let loose on us.

ON and ON

I knew trouble was close when I saw Heckle and Jeckle following Jimmy as he left the track. We planned to meet at his pub, take my money and skip town. Jimmy realized he was being followed and made a few nice quick zigzags and lost them. We met as planned and made the exchange. I asked him if he stuck to the plan. "Made a wager of my own, too, seeing how it was free money," he replied.

"You are so fucked, my friend. Get out of town as quickly as you can go." I cautioned.

"Born here, mate, I won't be going anywhere."

"Franklin Flanigan will be coming for his money," I told him.

"I'll take my chances, now piss off."

I have no idea what happened to Jimmy. I like to think he invested his money wisely, lived to a ripe old age, and Mr. Flanigan never entered the equation. (If you believe that nonsense, I have a bridge to sell you.)

I unfortunately do know what happened to Scotty. He was stopped right outside the betting station after collecting his money. I couldn't hear what was happening as I watched from a distance. Scotty was slapped around a bit, his money bag snatched from his hands and shoved in the back of a small cart. Two men, not Heckle and Jeckle, jumped into the back with him and continued to berate him. These were meaner-looking, no-nonsense men. It would only be a matter of time before they came looking for me. I had tried to safeguard Scotty earlier. "It's better to be safe; we are on the edge of being greedy," I said as I wanted to look him in the eyes. He would not hold my stare and kept looking away. He knew the consequences if he was caught, and he paid them. I was positive that I was or would be next on the list.

Both Scotty and Jimmy would sing like songbirds about my involvement. I was okay with that and had expected it.

I had previously booked my passage on a train to sea to train service traveling to Paris. The trip would take only three hours. I would cut it close and make my train with less than twenty minutes to spare. The service was called Southeastern Railway Company, the world's first internationally timetabled train-sea-train service. The service started forty years earlier, and the total trip back then had taken a little over twelve hours. With improvements to the harbor and additional tracks, the company reduced that time to three hours for my trip. I was somewhat jittery and nervous. I tried to keep a low profile while scanning the other passengers, looking for Flanigan's muscle. I didn't encounter any problems on the first leg of my trip. If Flanigan had even sent them, I had been fortunate to escape ahead of my pursuers. (I was sure he had.) I had taken a shitload of his money.

After arriving in Paris, I went directly to the Orient Express train box office. It was in the same station, which made it easy. The next departing train to Turkey was a week away. I considered taking another train elsewhere, anywhere. I could always come back to Paris after another adventure. But I had my mind set on enjoying the famous trip to Budapest and decided Paris would be adventure enough. A week was nothing. The Southeastern Railway Company ran one train a day from London to Paris. I planned to stake out the train station every day it arrived, watching as passengers disembarked, looking for men who might be looking for me. I could miss them, but I had an excellent idea of what to look for. Each day after I was sure I was safe, at least my money was safe, I did what I always did. Got drunk and tried to find a

ON and ON

woman to share my bed for the evening. (I love being twenty-two years old!)

I bought some new fancy clothes for my trip, I had to look the part. The Orient Express was a playground for the rich. I would not be riding coach. I planned on living it up. On day five, watching at the station, my worst fear came true. Franklin fucking Flanigan stepped off the train with five other men and my boy Scotty. At least, Scotty wasn't dead, but his face was beaten to hell. One eye was swollen shut, his big nose was swollen and broken, he was missing his front teeth, and he was not wearing his glasses. He had a new limp. He was a broken man with tiny beady eyes.

I would not be catching a train from Paris. I had already considered grabbing it further down the line, in Strasbourg or Munich. Now, my hand was forced. I left town that evening and headed for Munich. I tried to push the thought of Scotty's beat to fuck face out of my mind. I had gotten him into this mess, even if he was a stubborn non listening ass. I yelled "Fuck" out loud and told my driver to turn around and head back to Paris. Finding Mr. Flanigan would not be complicated; him finding me would not be hard for him either. I stood out from the rest of the crowd with my light complexion and light red hair. (Look for the drunk redhead.)

Flanigan would be staying in one of the four or five most exclusive hotels. I just had to find him before he spotted me. I didn't have a plan, but killing him seemed to be the line I was walking. I justified it by telling myself it was him or me. (Easy choice.) I had no idea how or where. I also needed to get Scotty away safely. (Fucking Scotty!) I knew Flanigan would be guarded. I also knew it was six to one against me. (I seemed to always be playing the long shot.) At least I wouldn't be dying, but I do feel pain, and I'm not a fan of that shit. (Hopefully not shot with arrows or scalped again.) I decided to buy a rifle and snipe his ass.

I found Flanigan in the third hotel I checked. He was having dinner alone while the rest of his crew, including Scotty, were eating at a table adjacent to his. Scotty was quiet, not engaged with the other men at his table. Seeing him sitting there, a beaten man, pissed me off. I found a young boy outside the hotel and paid him to walk by dropping a note into Scotty's lap. I didn't care if it was discrete or not. The others at the table were too busy to notice my note. The note said, "Be ready to run. Go to platform B as soon as it happens."

I made my sniper nest on the roof of the two-story building across from the hotel where they were dining. I calculated the best spot with the best view of the front door. If someone were to come to the roof, I was out in the open and would be seen immediately. I really didn't have another choice. The sneak attack I planned might sound cowardly, but so is hiding behind security guards. I lifted my collar to close off the cold air and counted my breaths as it formed small foggy areas from my face. I waited and hoped he would exit out the front door. I figured he wouldn't sneak out the back; he was the big dog, and the baddest do not hide. He had no reason to think he was being hunted. Franklin had no reason to fear anything as he walked out of the hotel's front door. He had no reason to believe he was my prey.

ON and ON

Mr. Flanigan exited through the front door as I predicted. He stood atop the stairs as one of his men went to get their transportation. He stopped to light his cigar, looking full and satisfied. I pulled the trigger, and the bullet entered through his left cheek and exited somewhere out the back of his head, splattering skull and brain across everyone standing anywhere close behind him. Time slowed as a dark-haired woman began to scream while wiping blood and gray brain matter from her face. It took several seconds for Flanigan's guards to react. It was utter chaos. Scotty was already running down the street, not looking back before anyone in the group knew where to start. I left the rifle on the roof, ran down the staircase, collected myself, made a quick but not hurried exit through the back door, and leisurely walked down an alley a couple of street blocks away but in the same direction as Scotty. It was a cold night, and I did not encounter anyone as I casually approached the train station. I saw him before he saw me. He was looking anxious and unnerved. I was wearing a trench coat and hat to not be recognized. It took Scotty a second to recognize me.

"Holy fek, you murdered him." He whispered to me as we walked away from the station. "Every gangster in London will be looking for ye."

"I think not. I just created a hole in the chain of command. A vacuum that will lead to many more murders before it's filled."

"You'll be a legend," Scotty gasped. "Do you think it's over? Will they come looking for me?"

"You should not return to London, that's for sure, but I don't think anyone thinks you pulled the trigger. And honestly, you are only here to identify me. Now, no one gives a fuck about me. We will travel to Munich together. I'll give you a fair cut of our winnings. Then I'll go one way and you the other." I told him. He didn't argue. Two days later, I was on my train to Turkey, and Scotty headed in a different direction. I never told him that I, too, had been greedy and had placed a separate bet myself in another betting station.

ON and ON

The Orient Express

I left Scotty and did not tell him where I was headed or inquire or care where he was headed either. I had used him, made him money, almost got him killed, saved him, and made him rich. He was on his own, and my adventures would continue without him. I was headed to Constantinople, now renamed Istanbul, Turkey, on the most famous train in the world. I typically do not like rich people; they are usually such assholes, but seeing as how I was going to be traveling with them, I figured I'd just be rich for a change. (Being an asshole came naturally)

The train had it all, including substantial sleeping cars, restaurants, and saloon cars that housed smoking compartments, and ladies' drawing rooms. With its Oriental rugs, velvet draperies, mahogany paneling, deep armchairs covered in soft Spanish leather, and fine cuisine, the Orient Express was unmatched in luxuriousness and comfort. For years, it attracted the elite of Europe's society, including royalty. (And me!) I would travel almost two thousand miles with scheduled stops along the way. The trip would last, give or take, about ten days. At each stop along the way, passengers were allowed to exit the train and explore that city. Vienna, Budapest, and Bucharest were our scheduled stops. The train was top-notch. Any and everything was available. There was a party every evening for the first-class guests. I met several lovely ladies and a few decent guys. I grew bored of the company after a few evenings. Most of the talk was about who they were, what they owned, what lineage they had, castle this, yachts that, all very tiresome. I wanted real people with honest conversations. The first class on the Orient Express lacked people with real-life experiences. What I needed was some exciting company.

My need for decent companionship was filled by one of our stewards. His name was Zaire. He was a lighter-skinned, well-educated South African man with a great sense of humor. He was a man who could navigate the pitfalls of elitist conversations and earn respect from the highest of bloodlines. He was great at his job and didn't take shit from any elitist. Zaire's enormous smile would pull you into whatever he was saying. He didn't blend in at all; instead, he wore his differences as a badge of honor. Zaire looked at me on the second day of my journey and asked, "Why are you on this train? You are very different from the usual travelers."

"How's that?" I replied.

"You look at me when you talk to me, and I do not see judgment in your eyes."

"What's to judge, a man doing his job exceptionally well?

He smiled his big smile and said, "When you're done pretending, come find me and the rest of the staff."

I took that to mean he was also bored of the company on the train. I had another night of pretending with the Duchess of something from somewhere. She was young and uninhibited. (God bless her.)

I found Zaire the next morning. We had stopped for the day in Vienna. I was the last one off the train; most other first-class travelers had grouped up for various excursions through the city. Zaire told me, "Go

ON and ON

eat something and return to the station in a couple of hours; I have work to do before joining you."

I ate an unremarkable but filling breakfast and killed the rest of the time as a tourist. The city was ancient, with famous landmarks and outrageous architecture.

I don't know what I expected, but what Zaire showed me was not it. We did not go to famous places and act like tourists. We began by sitting on the patio of a rundown cafe not far from the train station. The neighborhood was old and poor. Not ethically bound by any one race, the common ethnicity was hard-working peasant and poor. Drinks were served by servers who were pleasant and familiar to Zaire. He knew everyone and greeted each person with the same smile and genuine demeanor. He was like a mayor; he knew everyone, and everyone loved him. Soon after we arrived, musicians began to gather and play jazz-style music. It was wonderfully entertaining. The hours and wine passed quickly, and it was time to reboard the train. I tried to pay the bill, but Zaire would not hear of it. "This is my treat; you are my guest. Do not insult me by paying."

I had the feeling that I was being recruited for something, but I let my suspicions ease away; I was drunk and happy. I skipped dinner that night and went straight to bed. How Zaire made it through his shift is still a mystery. The next day, I thanked him for including me in his day and asked, "So what exactly can I do for you?"

He didn't even pretend to be shocked by the question. "Others on this train would have just assumed that it was their presence I was eagerly desiring from them. You see the world differently; I have a good feeling about you."

"You didn't answer my question." I persisted.

"It's what we can do for each other. We need more time and more wine for that conversation. After dinner tonight, if you can pull yourself away from your usual evening activities." He teased me. Smiling that smile at me. I spent the day watching the countryside through the vast glass window from the viewing compartment of the train. It was indeed a marvel. Both the window itself and the countryside.

On schedule, Zaire showed up at my private berth with three bottles of wine. I enjoyed our conversation and patiently waited for him to get down to what he wanted from me. "Have you ever heard of a place called the Modder River in South Africa?" Zaire began. I shook my head no, waiting for more information. "My family owns a large farm there. It's a beautiful place, and my family has been very successful."

"That would explain your education," I interrupted.

"Again, very intuitive." Then, he added, "Something fabulous and also dangerous and troublesome has occurred on our farm." he paused and then continued, "We have found gold, not just a little, but a substantial deposit."

"That's great luck, congratulations," I said skeptically. I still didn't know what this could possibly do with me.

"I need your white face." he blurted out without his typical smile. "In South Africa, blacks can own land, but we are a colony of the British government, and they will take our gold deposits and eventually the land, too. It's getting harder and harder to keep our gold a secret."

This should have felt like the email from the Nigerian Prince offering crazy money if you helped him by sending him your bank account info, but it didn't. It felt like an adventure to me.

"So, what do you need my white face to do?" Then I added, "How many other whitey's have you offered this to before me?"

Now, the smile returned but with a slight upward crook to it. He was amused. He laughingly said, "I've been looking for someone for six weeks, and you, my lucky friend, are the first."

"Lucky me?" I was smiling now, too. I didn't have the warning stop sign feeling in my gut. I believed him. Clearly, I'm not a fan of religion. A close second is colonizing governments who move in and push their policies and beliefs on a powerless, weaker population. (Like the Romans.)

"You will be the President of our gold mining company. The British will see you and not us. You appear semi-intelligent, look the part, and most importantly, I trust you."

"Good catch on the semi-intelligence." I smiled and quietly held in my excitement. I pretended to be pondering my decision. (No way in hell I wasn't going to South Africa.) "Fek it! I'm in."

We shook hands, and that sealed the beginning of a great friendship. It also began a profitable and soon-to-become deadly business venture.

I would have liked to have stayed a few more days in Istanbul. Still, Zaire was eager to return to South Africa. As soon as the train stopped, he resigned his post and began making travel arrangements immediately. The journey to South Africa would take roughly a month. We would sometimes travel by rail, horse, carriage, and even walk. I had never crossed the length of the continent of Africa. It was very diverse, from arid desert to bushland to dense jungle. I saw many animals I had only heard of from stories. Zaire hired local men as guides in places where the railroad did not travel.

Waking up fresh for the next day gave me an advantage that other men do not possess. It made my trip much less tiresome than Zaire's. I got up before everyone else to watch the sunrise and view animals I would have never seen. I was usually the last to retire for the night, also.

"Have I hired the devil to run my family's company?" Zaire inquired about twelve days into our journey. "You drink like a fish, never sleep, and do not appear afraid of any danger we encounter. Even worse, you look like you are on your first day of holiday every morning."

I laughed it off as usual; as you know, it's not the first time these questions have been asked. "I'm always eager to face the next day and hate the thought of ending a great one. What's to be afraid of? We live, we die. I want to experience every second of this life. I can sleep when I'm dead."

Not for the last time in our friendship Zaire looked at me like I had said some shit he had never expected. "You are much too young to be so philosophical. You will live longer if your fear increases a couple of levels." (Little did he know.)

I wish I could tell you about the great adventures that occurred on my trip through Africa. It'd be a better story if we encountered poachers, headhunters, common thieves, a romance with a beautiful tribal woman, stampeded by buffalo, snakes in my bedding, or any wild shit that could have happened. Sadly, it was uneventful except for the scenery and Zaire's personality. The trip was monotonous. We did have an entire pride of lions follow us for a few days. Their growls and roars were a little unnerving. I don't think I could survive being eaten by a lion? I've often pondered about my exact limitations of surviving different deaths. Anything where my body is destroyed seems to be the limit. Bombed, thrown in a vat of acid or a woodchipper, cremated, and eaten are my top guesses. After two days, the big cats moved along to easier meals.

Me and Zaire talked at length every evening. He told stories of his youth, as did I. We shared laughs and learned that we both spoke several languages, loved to drink, and adored women. (Common themes with my friendships.) We bonded on our trip, never had a disagreement, and ironed out the plan for my involvement in the gold mining operations.

Upon arriving at Zaire's farm, I was greeted with a hero's welcome and a feast in my honor. I met too many family members to remember them all. They all had that same ear-to-ear smile. I felt welcome. I felt needed. I felt included. I was determined to do my best to help this family and not become a victim of further colonization. The best plans are the simplest, Zaire's family's plan was to label me as the President of the gold mining company.

Before I continue, I need to give a brief history of South Africa in the 1890's and a little insight into the *gold* issue. The Dutch settled in the area two hundred years earlier, in the mid-sixteen hundreds. They were farmers. The Dutch were known as the Boers. They were intensely independent racist people who believed they were vastly superior to the native Zulus and hated the British intrusion.

The Zulu nation is the native people of the land. They were a fierce warrior class. Zulu also hated the British intrusion and had defeated the English many times over the last few decades. One famous and historically accurate encounter was made into a movie called *Shaka Zulu*; it's pretty badass. The British set up a naval base in the 1820s. South Africa meant very little to the British besides the importance of the strategic naval base. They tried to farm sugar cane but needed slave labor and found the Zulu uncooperative participants. Battles between the three groups fired up periodically for over fifty years. Each winning skirmishes against each other. Boundaries were eventually established, and most were good until gold was discovered. The British made a claim for the discovery of the leading gold area by saying a man named George Harrison discovered it on a farm in July 1886. This was a British attempt to give credit for the discovery to a white Englishman to justify claiming the gold fields as British. They wanted the gold for themselves and took the lands surrounding that farm. Once word emerged from a gold strike, the world flocked to share in the riches, just like in Alaska and California. Neither the Boers nor the Zulu were happy about the extra population. It could lead to political changes due to more white voters. Native South Africans who were classified as Zulu but were just simple farmers, like Zaire's family, owned land that could be worth millions of dollars if they were British or Boer but potentially stolen because they were black.

ON and ON

Understandably, the family was reluctant to put my name on the deed for their farm. It would have saved a lot of trouble and deceit, but white people had been fucking them over for years. I would not have done it, whether I was trustworthy or not. The plan was to present myself as the President of a prospective gold mining company. I would be the white face with mineral rights. I filed all the required documentation, and *exploratory* mining began. We waited six months to announce our readiness to bring some gold samples to market. During that time, me and Zaire became best of friends. We knew we needed to make it look like we still needed to strike gold; I used a few tricks I had learned from Jehon to set up a survey crew to show that the company was looking for possible dig sights. It became a game of keeping eyes looking where we wanted them to look rather than where we knew the gold was already located. We kept tight security on the farm's perimeter, and things progressed as we hoped.

The day finally came to bring in some samples. Our gold was 24 karats pure. (That's the best!) Word traveled fast, and in two days, I had several different investing companies visit me to entice me to sell my company to them. Selling wasn't an option. The family deserved the prosperity the mines would bring to them. We started selling small amounts of gold. For every one pound we sold, we stored ten. Too much gold would draw unwanted attention. This happened anyway when a group of Zaire's cousins decided to take some of the stored gold and sell it to a private buyer. Three things happened. They stole from the family, they got fucked on the price they received, and everyone for a hundred miles or more knew we had struck a colossal gold find. The four cousins were no longer trusted; there was serious talk of killing them. Fortunately, it was only anger talking. A two-year banishment to the crops and menial fieldwork was the punishment decided. They are still family, but probably never trusted again. They could keep the minimal amount of money they made by selling the gold they stole. Like a big fuck you to them.

British officers with a small garrison arrived less than a week later. They wanted access to our mines. I stood my ground and did not allow them entry. The commanding Major was furious. He was a small man who walked like he had a ginormous dick. His bottom lip protruded from his face like he just injected it with ten shots of Botox. He had eyes too big for his face and a huge but well-groomed mustache. I calmly informed him, "The British government has no jurisdiction over Zulu tribal land; my company has all mineral rights, and I am politely asking you and your men to please leave." He stared a hole through me, seething mad. He wasn't a person who was told no very often.

"Move or be shot."

"Go ahead and shoot; two hundred Zulu warriors will descend upon you and your men, and we can start another Battle of Isandlwana. How'd that one end up for you limey feks?" My anger was growing. "We have been expecting you greedy, thieving bastards, and we are prepared to defend what is rightfully ours."

The Battle of Isandlwana was a bloody annihilation of the British by the Zulu. A small troop did not want to fuck with the Zulu. The Major was trying to intimidate me, but it wasn't working. "Maybe I will just shoot you instead. You have worn out your welcome; kindly leave,

Major." He turned and directed his men to leave. The Major then said to me, "You have picked a fight with the largest army in the world. You and your dark friends are fucked!"

"I'll be sure to kill you first," I calmly replied.

After they left, I spoke to the leaders of the family. "They will be back, and in force, they will try to annex your farm and take it all." Everyone spoke at once. Finally, Zaire's voice was the loudest, and he calmed everyone down. "We have beaten them before, and we'll do it again. We have the advantage. They always underestimate us and see us as sub-human. That is how we win!" A roar of cheers arose from everyone but me.

Advantage or not, a war was not in the family's best interest. I had expected the visit from the major and had also spoken to a few other farmers (miners) in the area. We found out that the British were not unaware of the gold deposits. They had been quietly inquiring about the amounts being mined. Ours was one of the twenty-ish gold fields.

Another resource we had was the Boers. Zulu would have never even considered using them in any way, especially not as a resource. The Boers would have never considered working with the Zulu. Boers were the most prejudiced people I had ever encountered. Money or gold (which is the same) can relax people's views. I told the family, "I have spoken with several Boer gold miners." A hush fell over the gathered men. No family member had ever had a friendly exchange with any Boer. "We have a common interest and now a common enemy."

"You cannot trust them; they are evil people," Zaire exclaimed.

"The British will take your land and all the gold it contains. You can fight them, and you should fight. They will bring more and more troops and overwhelm you eventually. Or we can combine our resources with the Boers and possibly run them out of South Africa forever."

"Do you trust the Boers?" Zaire asked.

"Not in the least, but we can use them. The enemy of my enemy can be our friends. With the family's permission, I would like to talk with them. Essentially, my role here is done. You no longer require me as President of gold mining. I want to stay and fight side by side with my new family. I am sure an alliance with the Boers will benefit both of us." I left the meeting and awaited their decision.

There was much discussion, and an hour later, Zaire came to talk to me. "We really have no choice but to fight alongside the Boers. We will be equals and run our own attacks. We can fight our common cause separately but in conjunction with each other. Two battlefronts fighting the same enemy. We will not take orders from them."

The man I went to talk to was a Boer named Paul Kruger. He was The State President of the South African Republic. He hated both the British and the Zulu. Most non-Boars hated him right back. (Like I said before, money talks.) To avoid being overrun by the migrating gold miners flowing into his republic, he passed several taxation laws against foreigners. It took only one day to get a sit down with him. I got right to the point.

"I represent a Zulu gold mining family; the British are going to take their lands and most likely ambush and kill everyone living on them. I know they also plan on invading the gold mines in your region. The tactics will differ for your people but ultimately end with the same outcome. They will Annex your land and rig elections to have you removed, but as you know, the end results will be the same."

"Annexation is already in the books in London; all of South Africa is a goldmine, and they want it," he replied. He was a heavy man with devout religious ties. He was also a born South African and stubbornly patriotic.

"We, the entire Zulu nation, want to fight alongside the Boer's. The British have pillaged our great nation for long enough."

"Boers and Zulu fighting side by side will never happen."

"We propose two separate fighting fronts but with a common cause."

"I will run the idea by my generals. Come back tomorrow, and I'll have an answer for you." was his simple reply.

I didn't have to wait until the next day. I was eating dinner when three men came and sat at my table. Louis Botha, Jan Smuts, and Christiaan de Wet joined me and introduced themselves as Boer freedom fighters. They were interested in how I became associated with Zulus. I gave the three Boers some basic bullshit about gold being a great investment opportunity. I wanted to speak to them in terms they would understand. Social interaction between the races was at least seventy years in the future. A white man profiting from black laborers was much more believable and common. They were all for two separate fighting fronts. Like the Zulu, they would not take orders from anyone but an officer of the same race. Check-check so far. They had a completely different idea about how to fight the war, and I loved it.

Guerilla warfare is the term used today for how The Boers wanted to fight the Brits. We wouldn't gather troops and line up across from each other. (That type of war never made sense to me anyway.) They were planning to initiate small, quick attacks and retreat. The higher the ranking officer to be targeted, the better. Soldiers were doing their jobs; the plan was to cut the heads off the serpent. We would not win a conventional war. The British had too many troops. They had fewer officers. We wanted to kill them. The basic plan was to put fear into their hearts. Ambush them where they feel the safest. Keep them guessing, stagger our attacks, and keep them away from our gold mines. Each race could pick its own targets. I would be the liaison for the Zulu with bi-weekly meetings. I assured the Boer freedom fighters we would do our job, and we agreed on a vague war plan.

"We have everything west, funneling down into the cape, and they will start on the east. Two weeks from now, the attack begins." I told the family. "We need to scout for targets, gather every Zulu warlord, and find our best marksmen."

"Kwenziwa!" Zaire's uncle replied. (Loosely translates to done.)

We hit first. I insisted on being with the initial warrior group sent out to start the war. It was decided that our first target should send a message. Advanced scouting reports indicated the British ran early morning exercise groups on a regular schedule. *Amadevu,* the Zulu word for mustache, leads his company three days a week. Two other officers joined him regularly. I set up a small sniper nest near where the company trained periodically. Major Mustache's words had pissed me off; his arrogance and big dick-walking stance had made my mind up. I told him he would be the first to die.

It was a simple shot, and I did not miss it. My shot hit him dead center in the chest; my only regret was that he would not know it was me who shot him. Both accompanying officers were also impaled with Zulu lances launched by our warriors. Those nearby British soldiers gave a small chase until they ran directly into our remaining forces. Twenty or so British were killed, but not one Zulu had even a scratch. Message sent. An hour later, the Boers shot and killed seven British officers at a munitions depot that was encroaching on Boer territory.

Our two-front assault continued for over a year. The Boers took most of the credit (fine with us.) We confused and killed several hundred British officers. Paul Kruger had traveled to London a month after the rebellion had begun. He was there to use political efforts to make South Africa a sovereign nation. Kruger tried to make aliases with other world nations with no success. The gold in South Africa would be the most extensive deposits ever discovered globally. Not one nation was willing to fight England for it. We continued to ambush and assassinate. The family continued to mine gold and secretly stash and export it out of Africa. Even though we fought with the Boers against a common enemy, they still did not see the Zulu as equals. Every Zulu knew this fact. I did not even know or really care where the gold was going. The war would eventually end, and the whites would divide up everything.

Then, the British reinforcements arrived. Boat after boat filled with British troops began to collect, and men surged into the cape. Five hundred thousand extra troops were sent. Half a million men to fight against, maybe ten thousand of us. Overkill! They really wanted that gold.

One evening, I was approached by a single man. He was not dressed in an army uniform. He was tall and unafraid. He arrived on horseback and asked for me at the gate of our compound.

"You hate the Boers as much as we do. No one would believe Zulu and Boers were working together. Some still don't. Racist dumb bastards who can't see what's right in front of their eyes due to a lifetime of bigotry."

"And?" was my simple reply.

Shaking his head in disbelief, he continued, "I don't know how you did it, but you have brought the mightiest army in the world to its knees. Zulu warriors are in the British people's nightmares. Books are being written about their brutality and savagery. One day, I'd like to have a drink with you. Today isn't that day. We have a proposition, order your armies to stop killing British officers, and we will leave the natives and their goldmines alone."

I looked at him, trying to piece together who he might be, "I don't command anything here. I have no rank or position to give orders, but I can pass your message to the rightful ears." Of course, I countered, "I will need it in writing." Then I said, "My only goal here was to rid these great people of the plague of greedy vultures stealing what is rightfully theirs."

"Papers will be drawn up and delivered by messenger by noon tomorrow; please don't kill him."

ON and ON

"Don't send an officer, and he will be fine."

I turned and walked back to find Zaire. The counsel was unsure whether to believe what was being offered. There was never an alliance or treaty between the Zulu and Boers. Generations of war and hatred had not improved relations. Sure, we had fought a separate battle against a common foe, but the Zulu still hated the Boers as much as ever. I did not carry the same burden and decided to inform them of what the British had proposed to the Zulu. I waited for the promised papers. It was not a treaty but instead a letter commanding all actions against the Native peoples of South Africa to stop. Including military investigations into possible mineral deposits (gold). A leery Zulu council decided to stop the war games against the British and get back to mining gold.

I explained the Zulu position to the Boers. While not entirely happy to fight against the British alone, they seemed unfazed. "Fine, didn't need them anyway." That was the standard reply. I left without pointing out that the Zulu had inflicted as much, if not more, chaos as the Boers. It would have fallen on deaf ears anyway. Over the next two years, the Boers doubled down on warfare. Even with the added British troops. The Boers did not give a fuck. They killed at a higher rate. Ambushed entire colonies of men. Ratchet it up to include kidnapping and torture. It was much more than the gold. They felt the British were an invading force that needed to be repelled. Paul Kruger begged for a British withdrawal; instead, he got a group of men assigned to devastate the Boers at their fundamental core.

The British high command instituted a *scorched earth policy*. Instead of fighting just the Boer guerilla armies, they placed barbed wire around farms, which restricted cattle grazing; they ordered curfews to restrict population movement, and they rounded up families of Boer women and children. The families were placed in concentration camps, and over thirty thousand died of starvation and disease. Still, the hardest Boer men continued to fight and even began derailing train tracks. Eventually, the British prevailed, and a treaty was signed. The treaty was signed between the British and the Boer, not the Zulu. Gold mining continued, and Zulu land and gold mines were eventually confiscated. The native black South Africans again were left out of the money. Fucked again, as usual, Zaire's family was able to pull enough gold out of their farm and ship it far away. The last time I saw Zaire was on a cloudless, blue, sunny day as he and most of his family boarded a ship en route to Canada.

"You are unlike anyone I have ever met," he told me. "I cannot determine if you are extremely brave or insane."

"I am neither; I just needed a friend and an adventure."

I never saw them again. I left Africa soon after. With one hundred pounds of 24k gold! Estimated value of about seven million dollars today. (Not too shabby.)

The last Boers finally surrendered in May 1902, and the war ended with the Treaty of Vereeniging signed on 31 May 1902. The British offered the Boers generous terms of conditional surrender to bring the war to a victorious conclusion. The Boers were given three million pounds for reconstruction. They were promised eventual limited self-

government, granted in 1906 and 1907. The treaty ended the existence of the Transvaal and Orange Free State as independent Boer republics and placed them within the British Empire. The Union of South Africa was established as a dominion of the British Empire in 1910.

<u>Concorde</u>

While in San Diego with Ken, I met those college rugby players I told you about. During our session of drinking beers, they insisted I find a club team and play recreationally. It stuck in my head as something I should really try. So much so that I became a fan of watching the sport and traveled specifically to a few international games throughout the nineties. I returned to South Africa to attend the Rugby World Cup 1995. It was my first time on African soil in about a hundred years. (Since Zaire.)

While attending a game between the <u>Springboks</u>, the country's <u>rugby union</u> team, and <u>England</u>, it was obvious that most native South Africans in the stadium were cheering for England and not their own country, as the mostly-white Springboks represented prejudice and apartheid. Before the World Cup games, things began to change as the players were told to interact more with the fans, and the government made a PR push to be more inclusive. During the opening games, support for the Springboks grew among the black population. By the second game, the country came together to support the Springboks.

Nelson Mandela was the President of South Africa and used the World Cup and the Springboks to unite the races. His hope was helped when, in the opening game, the Springboks defeated one of their <u>arch-rivals</u>, <u>Australia</u>, the defending world champions known as the Wallabies. They then defy all expectations and defeat <u>France</u> in heavy rain to advance to <u>the final</u> against their other <u>arch-rival</u>: <u>New Zealand</u>, known as the All Blacks. New Zealand and South Africa were universally regarded as the two greatest rugby nations, with the Springboks the only side to have a winning record (20–19–2) against the All Blacks since their first meeting in 1921. The Springboks completed their run by beating the All Blacks 15–12 and winning the World Cup.

I tell you all this for two reasons: rugby is pertinent to the rest of this story, and I love it when sport becomes a significant part of helping solve social issues. (At least start the process.)

I decided to join a recreational rugby team after meeting a great guy named Salty Marshal during an after-tournament social. He was an Australian who had played basically since birth and was an ambassador for the game. He had played internationally and was now scratching his itch by playing on a club team (recreational) in Southern California. I will always remember my first rugby practice; if you don't know much about the game, it's a cross between football and soccer played without protective padding.

Grown men aged twenty to sixty were involved in a chaotic but somehow organized, spirited, controlled scrimmage. I kick myself for not doing it sooner. It is a glorious game (especially if you heal quickly.) There are many facets to the game. Playing the game is just one part. The camaraderie with your teammates is another. The social aspect is the glue in making the game so brilliant.

I was so nervous before my first game. I made so many rookie mistakes. I made terrible passes and committed several stupid penalties. I made a name for myself from my tackling. I didn't miss one tackle! I threw my body into every collision without regard for my physical well-being. (That's how my teammates and the fans saw it.) I was able to play without the fear of injury. (Huge advantage.) Hard, thunderous collision tackling would become my trademark. (I broke my collarbone several times, but it healed back nicely.)

I can't remember if we won or lost, but I remember my first after-game social party. After every game, the home team invites the visitors to their home bar or clubhouse. It's a long-held tradition. I have seen many fistfights on the game field. There is testosterone flowing and shit-talking being thrown around. There is never, I repeat never, a fistfight between teams at the social. I learned that rule in my very first season. I had made a tackle on a player who wasn't happy about it. A rugby tackle is taught to be more of a wrap-up of the player and drag him down to the ground. I tackled body to body to stop your forward progress. I landed on top of this guy, and while he was on his back, he threw a punch and hit me in the mouth. Because I was on top, I could easily rain down a few pouches back into his face. We were dragged apart with a few choice words exchanged between us. I had a tiny cut lip. He had a swollen shut right eye and a bloody nose. I was better positioned to throw punches than he was, and it showed.

I was in the bar before he came in. I tell a few of my teammates, "This fool is going to come in here and want so much more; I'm going to fuck him up."

"Slow your roll." one teammate said.

"You can't fight him now, that shit is over." another one added. I turned to look at him, wondering what he was talking about. I was pretty sure

ON and ON

the fight was only getting started. My opponent walks into the bar and loudly proclaims, "I'm looking for the bloke who dotted my eye!"

I stand up and push away from the bar counter and loudly reply, "I'm right here mother fucker!"

"Excellent, I've got a beer for you mate," he said, smiling.

What? You've got a beer for me? I instantly felt like the biggest asshole in the bar. I was embarrassed and somehow ashamed. I felt like everyone was looking at me. I walked over to him and accepted the beer, and he invited me to sit and chat. I liked him, I didn't want to, but I did. His name was Barry. He had a Caribbean accent and smelled like incense and the beach. He was a light cream color and wore his hair in short dreadlocks. He had an easy way about him that lowered my guard. (I liked his swollen eye, too)

"You don't tackle correctly," he started. "It's dangerous, more for you but also for all of us."

"It's not illegal," I answered defensively.

"Very true, but this is also recreational. Every player in this league has a job, most with a family to feed. You're out of control mate."

I sat quietly for a few moments. I hadn't thought about it that way. "I only have one gear. It doesn't hurt me, it feels fantastic to run through someone."

"I was chosen to instigate a fight with you; my team fears you. They would never admit it, but a few of our guys didn't play today because they think you're a dirty player. I personally am a fan. I wish you were on our team." He also explained the reason teams don't fight at the social. "It's called a gentleman's game. It's violence on the field with a strictly enforced code of conduct off the field."

I took what he said to heart and decided to tone it down, turning my nob down from a ten to an eight (It didn't last) I hung out with Barry the rest of the evening, and several players from both teams bar-hopped the next two days. I am still in contact with a few of those guys today. (Not in person, but a phone call or text now and then.) A month after I initially fought Barry, our teams played again. Before the game, I met him, and we exchanged pleasantries. I tell him, "Hope your calendar is open after the social; we have some exceptional entertainment lined up for the evening."

"Fuck yes." was all Barry said.

The game starts, and it's a close match. I made tackles but didn't hurt anyone. I catch a glimpse of something and feel a crushing elbow land across my jaw. It almost knocked me out. That bastard Barry had cheap-shotted the fuck out of me. While I see black figures float across my vision, my feelings are somehow hurt. I thought we were friends. I gather myself, get up, and have one single thought, find Barry. He's waiting for me. We square off and throw down. It's a very well-matched fight. Both of us landed and ate several punches. After about thirty seconds of all-out fury, fatigue sets in. We are both sucking air. And as quickly and as violently as it began, it ends with us both bending over, hands on our knees, bleeding, and smiling at each other.

"What the fuck was that all about?" I said in between heavy breaths.

"Couldn't let you walk around thinking I was a bitch and would just accept the black eye I've been carrying around the last month."

ON and ON

"I thought we were solid."

"We are now." He wanted to fight me that night after the game. The rugby culture would not allow it, so he waited until it was acceptable. I learned a lesson of being a true man, and I respected the fuck out of him because of it. (We had a blast that weekend together.) We played each other many more times over the years but never fought again. I never held back a hard tackle on him; he deserved my best.

Back to the social parties, we feed them and provide free beer to the team, their family members, friends, or anyone else who came to the game. Awards for the game are passed out in a "You played so well, now you're obligated to drink" fashion. Prank awards were also given for mistakes, like a lousy kick or stupid penalty. One team had a big pink dildo attached to a hat. It was called the dickhead award. The recipient was required to wear the hat for the evening.

After the food and awards, the real fun starts. There were always drinking contests as simple as a "boat race." Five or six contestants from each team faced off across from each other to see who could chug beers faster. The first two players start, and the next person can begin once his teammate has finished the entire beer, and so on, until one team finishes first. Other games include "tit for tat," where some form of alcohol is added progressively until the cup full of all sorts of spirits is either refused or not finished in one long drink.

The best part is when the singing starts. Inappropriate, sexually explicit, cleverly funny songs that had been passed down for generations, and every club had a new additional line to add and were sung for hours or until the bar closed or everyone was asked to leave.

Songs included *"Jesus don't play rugby"*, and every stanza is a reason why Jesus doesn't play, such as his dad fixing every game, Jesus only having twelve friends, wearing the wrong headgear, and playing in sandals. Another song was *"I Used to Work in Chicago"*. Every verse was the reason why he no longer worked there. Such as "switching the screen door/the lady wanted a backdoor" or a "floppy disk to a hard drive" or, my favorite, "changing the satin material asked about to felt". "Satin she wanted, felt she got! Ohhhh, I don't work there anymore!" Every song was silly, immature shit that was right up my alley. I loved playing and loved being included on the team.

I played with the Tusker's Rugby Club for five years. I traveled across America with this small team. Made friends with a wide variety of different types of people. Doctors, farmers, college students, and felons were all my teammates. We shared the game and also life together. We participated in not only rugby but community events and fundraisers for many local causes. The team had a knack for appropriate but also inappropriate nicknames. One guy was called psycho, another, turd in a punch bowl, piss-piss, quadzilla, bar-fly, Lando, Mexican Lando (he was Mexican and did look a lot like Lando,) muscle face, barnacle, AP (always pukes,) the Dr. of love (he gave himself that one,) and superfly. I never received a nickname; I was just referred to by the shortened version of my last name. (My nineteen ninety-five alias) I became close friends with a young man named Regor. It was one of my few friendships with a person who looked the same age as me. We drank and did stupid shit together and generally had a great time together. Regor was a bushy-headed Hispanic who was extremely athletic, fast, and elusive on the rugby field. We played different versions of the game; he was a runner and a playmaker, while I was the tackler (I heal quickly.) The yen and yang.

Regor never met a stranger; he would talk your ears off in a way that kept you interested. I lost him several times only to find him once sitting outside the bar talking with a group of homeless men and another time in the bathroom chatting up an old black bathroom attendant. He was supremely confident without being a dick. He always had a quick reply but somehow didn't rub anyone the wrong way. Our friendship was sealed when we both were selected to play in an all-star game. It was a weeklong trip. With him being young and me being me, we drank until sun-up, then played rugby all day and repeated with minimal sleep for the entire time. A couple of good-natured fistfights (not with each other), hustling a few pool games, both of us fucking it up on the field, and generally talking shit to everyone the entire week fortified our bond. Regor was selected as player of the tournament (rightly deserved.) I had his back and put double-digit players out of the game with thunderous tackles. (I also lead the tournament in penalty minutes. Yet, another less than humble brag.)

"I would love to go watch one of these games live someday," Regor said while we were watching a Six Nations rugby game early one morning. The local British pub opened early or stayed open late (depending on how you looked at it) to broadcast the live games being played in Europe. It was drunk talk, but I put a plan in motion to surprise him with a trip to England.

"Wouldn't that be grand," I replied with an overly fake Irish accent. Then we toasted our usual toast, "Titties and ass!" Which is touching the tops then the bottoms of our beer bottles together.

It took some doing, but I arranged for me and Regor to travel to Europe together; with Barry's help, I set us up with a rugby club just outside of Nice, in France. (BADASS!) Our apartment was steps from the sand. We would tour, play with our adoptive team, and work on the nearby golf course during the week. Our rugby improved by playing with men who had played the games their entire lives, and we had a great time. We both enjoyed playing golf. (I had played before, but Regor was brand new to the sport.) We spent every morning mowing the fairways, cutting limbs, fixing divots, and working on our golf swings. We spent two evenings a week at practice and playing almost every Saturday. Most of our free time was spent at the beach or in a drunken stupor. We surfed (you already know that it pisses me off that I am not a good surfer,) fished, lay around and drank under an umbrella, and just generally fucked off.

We took a short vacation and visited Paris to look at my road. (I am proud of that road.) Traveled to Spain to see if my vineyard had regrown. (It had, and I still have the deed.) I also stopped by the racetrack in London to place a couple of long-shot bets. (Lost both.) Of course, Regor had no idea why I chose those places to visit. Fortunately, he never inquired, so I didn't have to lie.

On one of our mini-vacations, we spent a weekend in Munich during Oktoberfest. I've never drunk more beer during one weekend. It was common to get separated from Regor. Usually, after a few more than

ON and ON

enough drinks, he would disappear to talk to anyone who would listen. Something or someone caught his attention, and he was gone for the entire first night. He was a grown-ass man, and I was not his chaperone, so go do you. In the meantime, I never had trouble getting into my own messes. I met several friendly Germans. Even attended a German funk band concert. The band was Boney M. I was drunk, they grooved, and Regor missed out.

Germans are a very unique people. Very rigid but also friendly. Most have a dry sense of humor and are bound to traditions of family and honor. The subculture is ultra-punk and rebellious but also encompassing and inviting. They all love to drink and fuck. (Hell, yes!) I found a drink that I've since learned not to indulge in; Jagermeister is a black licorice-flavored spirit that fucks me up. I refer to it as blackout juice. My last memory of that night is funking out to Boney M, dancing with a beautiful blond haired blue eyed punk *fraulein* woman. Strobe lights flashing, hundreds of drunk dancing Germans all around me…. then waking up under a staircase in a random apartment building the following day. It's very unusual for me to have a blackout evening. I was disoriented but knew the general direction of our hotel. The two-mile walk back to my room cleared my head, but I couldn't piece together anything from the concert to my stairwell sleeping arrangements. (I'd guess I had fun.)

Regor was passed out face down, naked, on top of his covers when I entered the room. He gave me no indication I was disrupting his sleep as I loudly walked into the room. After I took a long hot shower, walking back into the room, I found Regor dressed and furious. His lip was cut, and he had a giant three-inch open and seeping cut across his forehead.

"Where the fuck were you all night?" he hissed at me.

"You left me." I quickly explained.

"I was just around the corner for a few hours, talking to a couple of ladies. You always come to find me before we exit the area."

"It was almost six hours, and I did look for you. The crowd I was with walked about half a mile to a bar with a local band. What the fuck happened to your face? Looks like someone drew a big open mouth on your forehead." I said as I walked over to him to get a closer look.

"I got fucking hustled," he quietly admitted. "I was having an encouraging conversation with this Swiss girl; she was gorgeous. We decided to play a game of pool. A few drinks into our evening, a group of men began to hassle me. Nothing serious; I figured I could charm my way out of it. I got them to agree to a game of pool, and our usual loser buys the next round bet."

I wet a washcloth and began to try to clean up his wound as he continued. "I let him win the first game and brought back a pitcher of beer."

I interrupted him, "You didn't increase the stakes?"

"Of course I did. I was having fun, and they looked like suckas. We agreed to play for twenty dollars a ball. I ran the table." he meekly smiled.

"You're a dumb ass, your alone, no backup. What the fuck is wrong with you?"

ON and ON

"I was expecting you any moment, figured I'd just negotiate it down to a few beers. My opponent didn't have enough money to cover the bet and was pissed he had been hustled, especially by an American."

"You should have just bought your own drinks." I scolded

"You know damn well there is no fun in that, and don't be such an asshole about it. You have done the same thing many, many times."

He had me; we both had played the same hassle too many times to count. I had even been in several fights before I knew Regor, trying to pull the same bullshit. I didn't admit to any of that to him but instead just shook my head, showing him my crooked smile and lighted laugh, huffing out, "You look like shit; I hope it wasn't just one guy. I might have to rethink hanging out with some pussy who can't defend himself."

"My head hurts too much to laugh; there were at least three of them, four if you count the Swiss girl."

"You really got played. How much did they take?" I was beginning to get less concerned and angrier.

"Couple hundred bucks," he paused, then quietly added, "and my passport."

The busted head makes for a good story and, hopefully, a great scar. The lost money, while embarrassing, didn't matter at all. The lost passport was a huge issue. The wait time for another passport issued from a foreign country would probably be a few weeks. We had a critical playoff game next weekend. We needed to get back to France.

We decided to do the most logical thing, which in this case was to get drunk. Once inebriated, the ideas started flowing; like two drunk artists, we threw shit ideas onto a virtual canvas looking for something to stick. Reporting the stolen passport and assault to the police was the most intelligent and most reasonable idea, so we quickly nixed it.

I was sure this was not the first time these german hitmen (spicing it up a bit), I mean german teenagers (that's just to fuck with Regor) had ran this scheme. I hoped they would be careless or inexperienced enough to use the same bar to try it again, hopefully on an extremely handsome, redheaded, hilariously funny, humble gentleman. (Me!)

Regor wanted to stake out the bar, rush in full steam, and battle ram them into submission. I can't blame him; his pride was wounded, and he wanted blood. Being of a clearer head, I convinced him to be a little more subtle. I think he had at least a mild concussion and might not be as helpful in a fight as he was eager to engage. I needed the element of surprise. I would be outnumbered three to one, plus a super hot Swiss woman.

I needed to know who they were, so we sat at a sidewalk cafe across the street and not far from the bar. We had a good view of the entrance, and it was a beautiful sunny day. We ate a light lunch, had a few drinks, and people-watched. I immediately fell into my old habit of making up stories about the people who walked by. One couple was getting a divorce, a lonely-looking fella was looking for a building to jump off of, some were killing time before they had to go home, lovers meeting for a quick encounter, the usual make-believe bullshit. I still do it to kill time and entertain myself.

ON and ON

Finally, the Swiss girl arrived. She was not the runway model that Regor had described. She was attractive in a former druggy and leading a really had life kind of way.

"Her?" I questioned him.

"It was dark, and I was drunk, you're always busting my balls. Maybe I felt sorry for her." was his ridiculous reply.

"We need to work on your self-esteem or check your eyesight." I intentionally harassed him.

"Fuck off and go inside, I'll wait just like we planned.

I walked across the street, walked into the pub, and ordered a stein of local beer. I sat and took inventory of the place. Typical neighborhood bar. One pool table, a couple of small TVs, a jukebox, and a long counter with several small tables. The place was half full. Nobody paid any attention to me as I sat and sipped my beer. Swiss Miss was engaged in a conversation with another woman who looked about the same status as she did. Poor. The pool table was empty, so I chose a stick and shot a few balls by myself. Trying to be nonchalant, I hoped she would come by and engage me in conversation. If this was the con she was playing, I put myself in the middle of the trap. I played three games of pool with three men and won three more beers. She was finally close enough for me to offer her the third beer, with my excuse being I already had one. She accepted the drink and then disappeared. Maybe I played too well, but I had to win to keep the rights to the pool table. I had purposely missed a few easy shots to keep the games close and not draw attention to being a real player. I was sure I had caught her eye and was the perfect sucker for their next score.

After another game and win (Humble brag, again.) She walks back into the bar accompanied by three other men. Jackpot! One man asks, "What are the stakes?"

"Just a drink, if that works for you." I smile.

"Why is it that you Americans only want to play for alcohol?" He shittily says.

"Do you get a lot of Americans playing pool here?" I inquired.

"Some, let's play. Please don't bother trying to hustle me. We either play for money now or for drinks. Don't waste my time letting me win only to try to increase the stakes after making me think you're a terrible player."

I had to stop and think about what he just said. Why would he not be trying to hustle me? I was trying to figure out how to proceed. The man's name was Felix, and the Swiss lady's was Mila; both were incredibly nice.

"Drinks only are fine with me."

We played a very close game, and Felix beat me with a fortunate double-bank shot. I bought them each a beer and asked, "Run it back, let's play again."

I ran the table, so I didn't give Felix a shot after he failed to make a ball on the break. Felix didn't wait for me to make the final shot before he returned with a shot of my new nemesis, Jagermeister. I looked at remembering, well, not remembering, my experiences from the night before.

ON and ON

"I can only have one of these. I love them, but it really fucks me up. I call it blackout juice."

"Must be an American thing." Felix laughed. "We met an American in here last night, and he went from normal to passed out in three shots. He tried to fight everyone. Kept calling Mila his Swiss wife. He left his wallet and passport on the bar and disappeared."

"No fucking way. That is absolutely hilarious. What a fuck! Did anyone fight him?"

"No one wanted to beat his ass. He was really cool before he got wasted. He took a wild swing at Tommy over there, missed badly, fell, and hit his forehead on the corner of a barstool. We called for an ambulance, but he was gone by the time it arrived." Mila chimed in.

"You're not going to believe this," I told them. "That guy is my best friend. I'm only in here because he thinks he got jumped and robbed. He convinced me that you and Mila were running a con game to roll drunk Americans. He woke upbeat to fuck and missing all his belongings. I came in here to find you." I laughed.

"He said we beat him up? We hung out for four hours. Had a great time. I know all about you. Rugby players on a six-month trip to Europe. It won't be the first or last time someone has too much to drink. I assure you nothing like that happened. All his belongings are behind the bar."

"This is too good to be true." my mind was racing on how to fuck with Regor even more.

"He obviously needs to be punished," I told my new friends.

"Sounds like German and American friendships work the same way." Felix smiled. "What are you thinking?"

"He's eagerly awaiting me outside across the street, so we need to get another drink to discuss this more completely; drinks are on me." I declared, getting the bartender's attention.

Mila warmly stated, "His face looked terrible from his fall. Is he ok?"

"His face will heal; he's more shaken up about losing his passport. Considering he's hungover, has a three-inch open wound across his forehead, thinks he's stuck in Germany, and is still trying to piece together how his newfound friends stole all his shit,...he needs a lesson in the worst way." I laughed.

Felix proclaimed excitedly, "We could stage a fake fight between you and me outside the bar!"

"Or you and I stroll arm in arm down the street, like I'm leading you away to rob you." Mila interrupted.

"But then what? He is very embarrassed and itching to fight. He would immediately jump into our fight or follow us if we left the bar together. We need to use that against him." I said as if rubbing my chin like an evil cartoon character. (Just like my father used to do, damn.)

I remembered when I was eager to fight Barry after that rugby game, and he turned the tables on me and made me feel like a fool. He offered me a beer instead of a brawl. I told them the details of my idea. We all agreed it was what needed to be done.

ON and ON

I ran across the street straight towards Regor. He was up and met me before I got to the curb. I frantically told him, "I knocked one of them out, and Mila is ready to talk, but I may have really hurt Felix!"

His face went blank, "Who and Who?"

"The Swiss girl and the pool player who hustled your dumb ass." I shook my head at him. He had to have a concussion.

"Oh." was his sheepish reply.

"Come on, I need your help moving his body."

Regor stopped. "His body? What the fuck does that mean? The bar is fucking full of people. We can't just carry a body out the front door."

I had him; he went emotionally from action to panic. I turned my face away from him to hide my smile.

"Let's just leave, I can get a new passport. Let's go, fuck this," he said in a panic that almost made me feel sorry for him.

I did my best acting job and calmly told him, "He's propped up in a corner. There is a backdoor. Mila is retrieving your passport. I can't carry him by myself. You got me into this whole mess; stop being a pussy. Calm down and help me."

Regor followed me through the front bar door to a corner hidden behind the pool table. Felix was slummed down, sitting on the floor.

"Grab his shoulders, and I'll grab his feet. Be quick." I instructed Regor.

Regor reached to touch Felix, and then Felix slowly lifted his right hand, holding Regor's passport and wallet.

"You looking for these?" Felix said, looking Regor in the eyes and smiling.

"What the fuck!" Regor loudly yelled as he jumped back from Felix.

The entire bar was in on the gag, and laughter erupted as soon as Regor jumped away from Felix. He just looked at me as I handed him a shot of Jagermiester.

"This is the cause of all your troubles, my friend," I said, holding my own shot of blackout juice.

"I don't understand. "Regor stated, but I interrupted him before he could say something shitty about our new friends.

"You got fucked up, tried to fight everyone in the bar, fell, and hit your head on that barstool." I pointed to the innocent culprit, "You left your wallet and passport on the table and then disappeared."

He looked around, shame slowly fading across his face. Then a smile emerged, and his soul opened to all the facts in typical Regor fashion. He excitedly shouted, "Fuck yes!" He looked at Felix and Mila, panned his eyes across the bar at every standing looking at him, and proclaimed, "My most sincere apologies to all of you, but I won't lie to you; it'll probably happen again!"

Everyone laughed and cheered.

I surprised him with six national rugby tickets in early April that year. We watched France defeat Italy, then two days later enjoyed Scotland's surprise victory over an undefeated England.

"You got your wish," I told him during the first game.

ON and ON

"What did I wish for?"

"Back home, when we were watching at the pub, you said you would love to go to a Six Nations game," I reminded him.

"Musta been drunk," he teased me, "Fuck yes, I remember! So cool."

I had told him I received an inheritance, and money wasn't ever an issue. He insisted, "One day, I'll pay you back."

"It'll even out in the end." (It didn't.)

Our contract had us playing with the Nice team until mid-July. We finished and were ready to head back home. I had one more small surprise for Regor. I booked tickets to one of our favorite bands, The Beastie Boys, in New York City. I waited to show him our concert tickets until we boarded Air France Flight 4590, a Concorde passenger jet, from Paris to New York. He was genuinely excited, as was I. We sat in first class across the aisle from each other. The plane headed down the runway and then.....

The official report read:

While taking off from Charles de Gaulle Airport, the aircraft ran over debris on the runway, causing a tire to blow up and disintegrate. Tyre fragments, flung by the rapidly spinning wheel, violently struck the underside of the wing, damaging parts of the landing gear – thus preventing its retraction – and causing the integral fuel tank to rupture. Large amounts of fuel leaking from the rupture ignited, causing a loss of thrust in the left-hand-side engines 1 and 2. The aircraft lifted off, but the loss of thrust, high drag from the extended landing gear, and fire damage to the flight controls made it impossible to maintain control. The jet crashed into a hotel in nearby Gonesse two minutes after takeoff. All nine crew and 100 passengers on board were killed, as well as four people in the hotel. Six other people in the hotel were critically injured.

Again, tragedy struck in a seemingly beautiful part of my life. I had to be cursed. The hundred and eight passengers who perished didn't deserve to die; the six people in the hotel should still be alive. Regor was going to propose to his long-time girlfriend when we returned. It never makes sense. It's almost as if I'm not supposed to be happy. If my life intermingles too closely into someone else's life, they die. I'm not allowed to live a normal, happy life. It's just fucked!

I awoke still attached to my seat, but under a concrete pillar, my whole seat had been torn out, and the bolts had come loose. I was flung across what must have been a hotel hallway. There was a fire, but an eerie silence enclosed around me. All I could hear was the crackling of burning wood. I looked for my friend. I looked for anyone and saw nobody. I stumbled back towards the plane that was inserted into the building. The flames grew as I got closer. It was an inferno; the heat prevented me from getting close enough to enter. There were no screams, anyone inside was already gone. I would later learn that very few bodies were ever identified; everyone was cremated inside the fuselage of the Concorde. Their ashes were lumped together and bagged up for families to later collect.

I stared into the flames, my soul aching. Ten minutes ago, I was excited to go to a concert. I planned on a nap across the Pacific and a few cocktails. Now Regor was dead, and I was alone. Same bullshit all over

ON and ON

again. I was seriously injured but could not stay. (I'd be fine tomorrow.) I slowly dragged myself downstairs. I had to stop several times but eventually made it out into the sunlight. I turned and looked at the chaotic tragedy unfolding around the wreckage. Sirens of police cars, fire trucks, and ambulances scream towards the wreckage, filling the air with sounds of panic. Good Samaritans were rushing to try and help. News helicopters are already beginning to circle above. I took a deep, painful breath and started to shuffle away. I just needed to find a place to lie down for a moment. I was already feeling better, but not that much better. I was surprised when I felt a hand touch my shoulder. I hadn't heard or felt anyone close by. I turned slowly and looked up directly into the dark green eyes of my brother Jareth. (I knew it wasn't that fucking ring!)

About The Author

I am a high school physical education teacher in Bakersfield, Ca. father of four wonderful children, and for the majority of time, have been happily married for over 30 years. I have a lifelong love of reading. I love to travel and try every new beer within reach. I am an avid sports fan. Played rugby for over 20 years and support the LA Dodgers and Kansas City Chiefs. I have many hobbies including woodworking, gardening, golfing, hiking, fishing, and snuggling on the couch with my dogs while watching TV (especially good sci-fi and British crime dramas.) And my newest hobby being an author. I enjoy the perspective of history and I find historical fiction extremely limitless.

I'm adding a few free chapters of the next book in this series, please continue reading Jareth. The next book is due to be finished in early 2025.

Preface

68 A.D. Caladonia. The day of the invasion

Fabius sat upright and ridged as his steed Dux peered over the wet, soggy swamplands. The sky was a clear misty blue, and looked as if he could see forever. Dux is as much in charge as himself. They had been together for over five years, and Fabius loved her more than any human in his life. He had a discontent with most people. A better explanation was that he damn near hated everyone. He had no reason for his distaste. A more precise definition might be that he just didn't give a fuck about anyone but himself. No one had ever fully understood his inner soul, even as a child. He liked to think that Dux knew him. He realized it was a fool's wish to believe a horse could know his inner thoughts. But, it gave him a sort of peace to trust in Dux. As they waited, the horse swatted flies away with her tail. She never grazed while on duty; she knew the day's importance.

Fabius had a burning desire for perfection. He hated men who half-assed their duties. He would not and could not abide sloth. His Legio (legion) was the finest in these Scottish territories. He commanded with an iron fist, which brewed hatred but also respect.

"I'll take obedience and fear," he said in a low voice to Dux, who snorted as if reading his mind and agreeing to his words. After almost a year of chasing, fighting, and hopefully today conquering these idiot

ON and ON

Highlanders, Fabius was tired. His mind was always racing, so he never slept well. Thinking of his next move. Who could be bought, who could be manipulated, who needed to be killed? Killing was always the easiest and gave him the most pleasure. Not the actual death, but the plan, the scheme, the chess game of being three moves ahead in the game before his victim even knew they were playing. His plans usually started with killing someone, but unfortunately, most times, simple blackmail or well-intended threats sufficed.

Fabius would someday be Magister Militum (the general in charge of the southern Roman army.) Today, however, he was just in charge of gathering food stock for the legion—a slap in his face posting. Any fool could take livestock and grain from the peasants. He had to admit that his ambition pushed him out of favor with the commanding officers. His rise in the Roman army had shifted. He started in a higher-ranking position than most due to the prominence of his family's name. His father was a whisperer to the Roman senate, kept many secrets, and was owed favor from essential men.

"The apple does not fall far from the tree," his father repeated many times to Fabius while growing up. They each saw the world as what it could do for me instead of what they could do to improve the world. Making the world a better place was so cliche; such nonsense Fabius had pushed the thought away times. I'll do what's best for me. What benefits me is his lifelong motto. Using this motto, he stepped on and over many better soldiers than himself on upward movement in rank and stature. His best assignment, which used his gifts and talents, was Quaestionarius, the interrogator or torturer. He knew he was a narcissist, even knew the definition of it, but as one, he didn't care. He wondered why others put themselves last. His needs and desires were always first.

Inflicting pain and suffering upon others was of no consequence to him. It's the same as squashing a spider or scorpion that might bite him later if it wasn't disposed of. Screams and pleas for help fell upon deaf ears unless the information was helpful to Fabius. Often, it was beneficial. Even on this cloudless day, he fondly remembers Boudica, a homely, slovenly man with intelligent eyes. Fabius had no reason to continue the torture. He had extracted all he needed to know, but as Boudica screamed and pleaded, Fabius felt less and less compassion. His compassion gage was always near if not completely empty. He found enjoyment in Boudica's pain. It made him sexually excited. He had used this wonderful memory several times already. It might be time to make a new one.

His mind quickly moved on to his newest situation. He had overplayed newfound information about a general sleeping with another high-ranking official's wife. He quietly passed on this damning information to the right ears. He was promoted to Hastatus Prior, a jump generally taking a lifetime. Unfortunately, the ears to which he passed his information were not as quiet as himself, and he drank too much, whispering his secrets to many ears. Soon, everyone knew Fabius was a man who was not to be trusted. Hince was standing on this hill with Dux, preparing to rob meat from the poor.

ON and ON

Chapter 1

2000 France

I was utterly speechless. Was it him? How could it be him? If it was Jareth, why wasn't he smiling at me? Why was he a couple of feet out of my reach? I wanted to embrace him. I hadn't seen my brother in over two thousand years. I could have said, "How?" but I knew the answer. I stood there silent, not knowing what to say. Finally, I muttered, "Is it you?"

"Of course, it's me; who else would it be?" he stoically answered.

Tears ran down my face. I felt absolute euphoria, but Jareth did not match my emotions. He was stone solid, like a marble statue, unmoving and unemotional. It's like he was somehow mad or upset with me. (What the fuck had I done?)

"What?" I exclaimed loudly. "Why are you just staring at me?"

"You once told me you would never leave me," he stated bitterly, like a boiling kettle of hate.

"Are you fucking serious? Last time I saw you, you were damn near decapitated and burned into a black shell. I examined your body. You had been tortured and mutilated," I added with emphasis. "The Romans fucked you up, I thought you were dead. Everyone was dead."

"Dad said you fled, turned tail, and ran like a coward. Ran like a bunny being chased by a wolf, he would always say." Jareth said it in a mockingly harsh Scottish accent. It was either meant to hurt me or impersonate our father. He accomplished both. Now, I was pissed. It's funny how my jubilance could change so quickly. We had not seen each other for centuries. Still, before we could even discuss the impossibilities of our existence, Jareth had to unburden himself of his anger toward me. He somehow felt I had wronged him. Carrying that pain for this long must have been horrible. My anger quickly ebbed as I stared at him.

"Dad gave me this stupid ass ring and told me to leave," I said as I held my hand out to show him the ring. "I would have never run; you know I was angry about everything; I would have never run. During the battle, I remember being stabbed but awoke unharmed." I stopped to let that sink in, then exclaimed louder than intended, "Dad? Wait, dad survived? Is he like us?"

"No, he died about twenty years after the original invasion. He never would speak your name again until the night he died." he then quoted my father, but this time in a much gentler tone.

"It skips generations, then will reappear. My great-grandfather told stories of relatives who would return looking the same after fifty years. Everyone dismissed him as crazy or creating ghosts. His stories were considered folklore. Promise me you will find your brother, promise me! It might take you a lifetime but leave here and find him. I suspect both of your lives will be long ones. Forgive him; he didn't know; I should have told him."

"That was Dad's last breath. Years of refusal to discuss anything, he unloads everything in five seconds and dies." Jareth says, slowly shaking his head. "It took some time to decipher what he meant. I

ON and ON

remember The Romans coming to our home. What they did to us, I will never forget. I have a blank space from being held and made to watch the immoral acts bestowed upon Mom and the others. I have used that anger to fuel me, to define me every day since. I have no memories of what they did to me besides a few punches and being restrained. I'm sad to say I awoke feeling grand, looking into Dad's face. I had been unconscious for two full days. Dad had buried our dead and cleaned what was left of our home." he finished.

"We need to move away from here. I need a short nap to heal, " I interrupted.

"Fine." was all Jareth said, turning and walking away. I followed.

Chapter 2

Four months before the Roman invasion.

Jareth knows they can't win, but his family has decided to take as many murdering, thieving, invading Romans with them to hell. He tried to convince his dad and brother to stay fight at the farm, but both pig-headed men insisted on representing the family where everyone could witness their bravery.

"Fecking fools!" Jareth yelled at both men as they left for battle early that morning.

The entire family had worked nonstop for months preparing for today's ambush. Livestock carrying most of their grain stores had been led many miles away. Young Sebastian, a barely six-year-old thin and fidgety boy, had been left as a shepherd to guard it. Jareth has his most significant doubts about him. Sebastian is his first cousin's son and has been left in his care while his father is away fighting.

Months ago, Jareth recommended that the entire clan leave everything behind. Wait, this nonsense takeover out in the hills where only goat trails lead.

"Pale's Gorge contains all we need. The entire clan can live there for years, possibly never to return," he had begged them. He bitched and stubbornly suggested it so many times he was finally able to convince

ON and ON

his dad, brother, two uncles, and some cousins to travel three full days to take a look.

"What's the difference where you lay your head at night? At least it will still be attached to your body. We can rebuild our homes here. There is grass for feed and clean water; we can completely rebuild," he pleaded.

"I won't run from this fight," his father gruffly stated.

"I'm not a coward," exited his brother's lips.

"Our clan will be the laughingstock of the entire area," one uncle laughed.

"I won't do it!" bellowed a cousin.

Jareth looked at them all, outnumbered, out stubborned, and out loud, saying to them, "Your bravery is commendable. You all know we can't win. The best scenario is to come home with missing limbs. We will still be under the Roman Yolk. The proverbial mirrors you won't be able to look into because you're afraid to see a coward staring back should be exchanged for the reflection in your wives and children's eyes staring back at you because you chose to stay and protect them from the death, enslavement, and rape that will surely happen when you throw your selfish bodies against Roman blades!"

Jareth walked the entire thirty-six hours back to the farm. His anger seeped from his soul. He walked as if in a dark tunnel, seeing nothing but rage that yelled at him from all sides. The arrogance and lack of sense from his family members encompassed his every thought. His despise for the invading army was somehow less. Armies do what armies do, and soldiers obey orders. His elders could not see beyond their prideful selves.

During hour thirteen or fourteen, his mindset began to change. A realization of logic slowly pushed out his emotional connection to the problem and started taking over his thoughts. He slowly exited his mind's dark tunnel and saw a full harvest moon. The night was clear, and the sky was full of stars, the most fantastic, beautiful space with too many specks of light to count. So were the options to save his family. He only had to think bigger, see the problem differently, and speak a language the Roman's egos would not expect to be reading. The vastness of the horizon aided in opening his mind. Ideas suddenly raced in and out of him: maybe we could do this, or perhaps this concept might work. From one plan to another, a small idea slowly grew. He would have only women and children to fight. Traps and surprise would be their only hope.

Many years ago, he had overheard a stranger talking to the feed store owner.

This stranger had traveled from a land far away and was physically with his hands describing a new weapon he had seen used in a battle that this man was running from. Jareth reached deep back and tried to recall the exact memory. It was a bow, but held against the shoulder horizontally, not up and down. It launched small arrows. He vaguely remembered the man saying it looked like a cross.

ON and ON

Chapter 3

Caladonia

Dux and Fabius watched as arrows darkened the blue sky. A few painted men dropped to the earth, and others snuck away. Not as many as in other pre-encounters Fabius had observed. They were brave men, Fabius had to admit, but also ignorant. Somehow, they believed their blue and green-painted chests and faces would shield them from bolts and lances. Like their god's lives inside the paint and on the brushes used to apply the useless coating would wave away all harm. He had seen the same tactics used before. Roman soldiers had been briefed to understand why savages used such emboldening measures to get a slight edge and the intimidation that made them feel invincible. Giant men from much further north had put fear in his heart, looking like giant hairy beasts lining up to eat him in his first encounter with such nonsense. Those peasants bled and died like all other men in history, but they did fight savagely, and our forces only won the battle due to sheer numbers. This minor skirmish would not be a problem today.

The open, muddy clearing chosen to eliminate the so-called North Men appeared ready for guests. Trees surrounding the meadow were filled with crows, ravens, and every other hook-beaked bird that resided in the area, like a stadium filled waiting for the big game. Vultures circled above, ready to dive bomb into the remains of unfortunate souls, giving their meaty bodies for the benefit of everyone's dinner. Fabius casually wondered how these creatures knew what was about to happen. It was as if an alert had been signaled to every scavenger that a meal was being prepared for all to attend.

Twelve men rode in two rows side by side. Red capes whipped as they rode. They wore shiny gold helmets with a single line of feathers in the center running midway down the length, mid-forehead to mid-neck. The line of feathers is called a plume, signifying these Legionary soldiers' rank. All twelve men were nearly identical in height and weight. All twelve horses were as similar as siblings. Fabius made sure all these small details were exact. No conversation was allowed. Each man and beast were drilled continuously and knew their role. Two extra men, not regulars in his Legion, pulled a wooden cart each. They were the meat and supplies collectors, not Roman soldiers, but slave labor, attached to kill, butcher, and transport the meat needed to feed the army. They were nasty, foul men. Unkept, ugly, and smelled like death. Fabius instructed them to follow far behind and only arrive on his signal. He could not stand the sight or smell of them. Both men wore threadbare, wholly wool coverings and some sort of skirt, possibly a kilt. Blood from butchering stolen cattle covers their faces and clothes. Huge oxen pull their carts.

Fabius started his round-up shortly after the first arrows from Roman longbows were loosed. There would not be much to see on today's battlefield. His role was to kill and steal. The people of these god-forsaken hills meant nothing to him—ants in an anthill. Burn the entire colony for all it mattered to him. Four small farms containing a few sheep, a small amount of grain, fifteen or twenty chickens, and very few cows were all he had gathered so far today.

ON and ON

"How do these fools survive?" he thought to himself. He could have left with just the foodstuffs, but he instructed his men to burn all the huts and barns for no other reason than that he was bored and liked to watch the flames. He also felt that it would dishearten any survivor who was walking home to see the smoke and know the Romans were not someone to fuck with.

Old women and children stood watching with dirty sour faces and hateful eyes; Fabius had less than a "Fuck them" to spare.

Entering the fifth farm, Fabius felt discontent—just a tiny poke to his intuition. The farm was more significant than the others but also very well-kept. The road to the farmhouse was lined with large oak trees, trimmed, and pleasing to observe. The path had been excavated, not merely run over by carts creating two small ruts on the top of a hill. Boulders ran the pass length like ancient gargoyles looking down from above. Fabius's mind saw a fortification that could be defended with a minimal force, but he quickly dismissed the idea. Why would farmers need such advanced protection?

His thoughts were rudely interrupted when a large, fit young man appeared just beyond a fallen tree blocking the road. Jareth stands tall and unafraid.

"We have no wish to fight you. We will bring you a tribute of half our cattle and grain. We only ask to be left with enough to survive until the next harvest and our buildings not to be burned down."

These peasants' arrogance amused Fabius. He decided to play along, but he also decided right then to kill everyone and build the most enormous bonfire he had ever built.

In a very light-hearted voice, Fabius replies, "To the victor, go the spoils, but I suppose if you give us all of your livestock and grain, I could be persuaded not to kill everyone and burn only half of your dwellings." Fabius thinks he is clever, and this lad has no idea who he's dealing with; his amusement quickly turns to astonishment as the man in front of him raises an odd-looking weapon and fires a small arrow directly into his chest.

"A crossbow? I've never seen one in this land," is his immediate thought as the bolt lands, wedged just below his right collarbone. Fabius falls from Dux, and then the world around him explodes. The decorative stones above Fabius and his men suddenly roll down the hill towards them. Bolts of sharp wood find the soft flesh of his legionnaires, and five men fall off their mounts, crushed by falling stones. In a panic that no amount of drills could have prevented, horses scream, men yell directions, and everyone dead set on exiting the funnel of death. The walls of the passage are not steep, but with dirt and stone raining down, straight through is the only escape route. As they exit, the ground in front of them, which they are riding directly into, opens. A tarp covered by light dirt and debris opens to reveal a trench with two-foot-long sharpened poles pointed directly at the horses riding nonstop onto them. The haste with which the riders escape the falling rocks prohibits any other safe path, and the first evading riders fall right into the next trap. The horses cried a terrible cry, scrambling to un-wedge the vampire stakes lodged into their flesh, throwing their riders onto the next set of sharp poles. More than half of his army is dead. Fabius has an arrow sticking out from his front

ON and ON

and back. The pain is immense, but still, the anger at himself burns higher.

"I've let my arrogance underestimate these simple farmers," he thinks. "Dux is the only clear-headed individual in a storm of chaos." His love and admiration for her grows inside him. Using all his strength, Fabius climbs on her back and uses his instincts and training to assess the dire situation. More than anything, he is embarrassed. For a man who strives to be the best, he has been caught with his pants down and will face ridicule and drop several ranks due to this failure. Dux cautiously sidesteps another pit of wooden spikes as Fabius uses his long swords to uncover the tarp and reveal the death trap; he can't afford to lose another soldier. He shifts his body weight and tries to sit high in the saddle.

A light mist started to fall from a clear sky containing just one cloud. The sun was partially blocked, casting a shadow over the circus of carnage. The sounds of falling earth and death gave way to an eerie silence. It was just the eye of a hurricane; mayhem continued all around the small farm. Not five miles away, men are impaled by lances and stampeded under a calvary of horses. More dangers await him and his men beyond this road to the farmhouse. Fabius takes a moment to collect his thoughts. The fit young man has disappeared to unleash more damage on his troop elsewhere. He has no choice but to push forward.

"Regroup on me," he yells loudly to his men.

Jareth and his army of women and children prepare for round two. The surprise attack has fared far better than anticipated. He had hoped to disable two or three Romans. They have killed seven. More traps have been set. Several other pits have been dug strategically, awaiting their victims like a trap door spider awaiting unsuspecting insects to fall in. A rope covered with leaves is on stand-by between two trees, and it is to be pulled at the last minute by seven-year-old cousin Rory, who is hiding camouflaged just in case any Roman charges his way. He has a sharp kitchen knife and has been instructed precisely where to stab it. Rory is a deadly hunter. Jareth has no doubts about his abilities.

Other family members are also strategically hidden and have been told only to reveal themselves if needed. Some with the crossbows Jareth has made for them. Each bow took several days to fashion and test, but all are deadly. His sister-in-law is sitting on the cellar floor facing the door against the far wall; if she doesn't hear the code word before the door is opened, she is to fire at the first person entering through the door. Multiple booby traps are awaiting the unexpectant Romans. Jareth hopes his new language is still unreadable.

ON and ON